पुरातत्त्व

PURĀTATTVA

Bulletin of the Indian Archaeological Society

No. 24 1993-94

Editor

K. N. Dikshit

Assisted by

S. Ganesh Rao, Ashwani Asthana and B.S. Hari Shankar

D.K. Printworld (P) Ltd.

New Delhi

Cataloging in Publication Data — DK

[Courtesy : D.K. Agencies (P) Ltd. <docinfo@dkagencies.com>]

Purātattva : bulletin of the Indian Archaeological Society, no. 24, 1993-94 / editor, K.N. Dikshit ; assisted by S. Ganesh Rao, Ashwani Asthana and B.S. Hari Shankar.

p. cm.

Includes bibliographical references.

ISBN 8124602999

1. Archaeology — India — Periodicals. 2. India — Antiquities — Periodicals. 3. India — Civilization — Periodicals. I. Dikshit, K.N. II. Indian Archaeological Society.

First Published in 1994

First Reprinted in 2005

ISBN 81-246-0299-9

Price for volume 24 (1993-94): Rs. 800 US $ 40

Reprint authorised by

Indian Archaeological Society

New Delhi - 110 016

Purātattva is published annually.

Manuscripts (whether in the form of articles or notes or book reviews) offered for publication should be sent to the Editor, Purātattva, Indian Archaeological Society, B-17, Qutab Institutional Area, New Delhi - 110 016.

Published and printed by:

D.K. Printworld (P) Ltd.

'Srikunj,' F-52, Bali Nagar

New Delhi – 110015

Phone : (011) 2545 3975, 2546 6019 Fax : (011) 2546 5926

E-mail : dkprintworld@vsnl.net

www. dkprintworld.com

PURĀTATTVA

CONTENTS

Pages

Obituary

Editorial

ARTICLES

Vedic and Harappan Culture: New Findings — 1
Navaratna S. Rajaram

The Iron Age in India: the Beginning and Consequences — 12
Dilip K. Chakrabarti and Nayanjot Lahiri

NOTES AND NEWS

A Report on the Discovery of a Palaeolithic Site Near Katra, Udhampur District, Jammu — 33
R.K. Ganjoo, Satish Safaya and Pankaj Lidoo

A Preliminary Report on the Faunal Remains at Padri : A Harappan Site in Bahvnagar District, Gujarat — 35
P.P. Joglekar

Excavation of Tisseru Stupa (Ladakh) — 39
R.C. Agrawal

Anangpur Fort: The Earlier Tomar Settlement near Delhi — 41
B.R. Mani and I.D. Dwivedi

A Report on IOC Organised National Conference on Pollution and Historical Monuments — 43
Indian Archaeological Society

BOOK REVIEWS

Shiv Kumar Sharma: Painted Scrolls of Asia — 46
S.P. Gupta

Vijay Kumar Malhotra : Kamal-Śāśvata Sanskratika Pratīka (Hindi) — 46
S.P. Gupta

Shail Pradhan: Bhārtīya Kala me Vaishṇava Paramparā — 47
K.N. Dikshit

Sudhir Kumar Trivedi : Madhya Bhārat kī Pratihara Kālīna Kalā tathā Sthāpatya (Hindi) — 47
Shashi Asthana

INDEX TO PURĀTATTVA NOS. 1 TO 23 — 48

Obituary

Walter Ashlin Fairservis, Jr.

17 February 1924 — 12 July 1994

Walter A. Fairservis, Jr., the senior American archaeologist working in South Asia, passed away at his home in Sharon, Connecticut on July 12, 1994. He had retired a year ago as a professor of anthropology at Vassar College where he had been Chairman of the Department of Anthropology and Sociology and head of their Asian Studies Program for many years. Fairservis was working on his report on the Allahdino excavations, the only remaining obligation to his distinguished record as a field archaeologist. His colleagues prepared a festschrift for Walter's South Asian Archaeology Studies. This has a biographical statement of Fairservis, rich and varied career, which is summarized here.

Raised in New York and educated at number of institutions of higher learning, principally Columbia University, the University of Chicago and Harvard University, Fairservis was determined to be an archaeologist from his childhood. This led to a long lasting relationship with the American Museum of Natural History in New York City and they supported his first archaeological project in Pakistan. This was known as the Second Afghan Expedition which worked in Pakistan and Afghanistan from August 1950 until May 1951. It was during this period that he excavated Kili Ghul Mohammad and Damb Sadaat, along with other sites, and completed a survey of the Quetta-Pishin valleys. This was published in his 1956 monograph *Excavations in the Quetta Valley, West Pakistan.*

Fairservis was widely published in diverse themes in archaeology and anthropology. His *Threshold of Civilization* was an exploration of the human psyche and an experiment in archaeological reasoning. But he also wrote on the archaeology of China and was the first director of the renewed excavations of Heirakonpolis in Egypt.

In addition to being an archaeologist and anthropologist, Fairservis had a career in the theater. He was a member of Actors Equity of long standing and also an accomplished playwrite with many credits to his name.

Gregory L. Possehl

PURĀTATTVA

Number 24 **1993-94**

Editorial

It gives us great pleasure to present to our readers the Purātattva No. 24 (1993-94). It is coinciding with the World Archaeological Congress–3 being held at New Delhi from 4th through the 11th December 1994.

The present volume contains two very significant papers — one by Rajaram , a distinguished scientist, who was formerly in the Advisory Committee of the NASA in USA, and the other by Dr. Dilip K. Chakrabarti, presently teaching in the Cambridge University, U.K., along with Dr. (Mrs) Nayanjot Lahiri, a lecturer in the Delhi University. The former concerns the Harappan or the Indus-Saraswati Civilization and its relationship with the Vedic Civilization, a subject on which so many scientists are working in USA, all reaching to the same conclusion that the Indus-Saraswati and the so-called Vedic Aryan Civilization are only the two sides of one and same culture-complex datable to the 4th and 3rd millenia B.C., or even earlier. The latter article deals with Iron Age in India in the light of ancient technologies, contributing technologies in the remote villages as well as the present day high technologies. Its database is extremely solid. The Iron Age in India, the authors suggest, may have started during the period bracketed between the 14th century B.C. and 13th century B.C.

There are, of course, the regular columns of 'Notes and News' as well as 'Book Reviews'.

We take this opportunity of thanking our chairman, Dr. S.P. Gupta, for his guidance, help and encouragement in our efforts to bring out this volume. We also thank Shri S. Ganesh Rao, Ashwani Asthana and B.S. Hari Shankar for their most valuable help in going through the manuscript as well as the proofs.

— K.N. Dikshit

Vedic and Harappan Culture: New Findings

NAVARATNA S. RAJARAM

The results on the history and chronology of ancient India and the world that I am going to present here may appear very radical, but I am conservative. The dates I give will seem ancient, but I am reasonably confident that when they are revised, as they surely will be revised, the revision will be upwards, to earlier dates. But I would like also to note the difference in approach that will be presenting that distinguishes what I call the Indo-American school that is just beginning to emerge mainly in the United States and Canada though it is not by any means limited geographically.

What is this Indo-American school? I can probably best explain it by contrasting it with the approach followed for more than a century in India and the West, one which will call Indo-European. There is now a critical mass of workers in America and Canada interested in the history of ancient India, and the ancient world, so we now can claim to have a distinct school of scholars. When I use the phrase Indo-American it applies to those workers who are predominantly American trained and follow a particular approach. It is by no means a national or geographic designation. Some of us are Indian born, some of us are American, some even Europeans but we all follow a line of investigation quite distinct from the Indo-European school. Many, perhaps a majority of Indologists in American universities are also very probably Indo-European by my description. Among members of the Indo-American school, I count David Frawely, George Feuerstein, Subhash Kak, Harry Hicks, Jim Shaffer and myself among others. You will note that we are not distinguished by nationality. The question all of you probably have is how are we different? will begin to answer that question first by a brief portrayal of the Indo-European school as I see it.

The Indo-European school, whose version of ancient history is what dominates the history books today began a little over a century ago. Its patron saint is Frederick Max Müller; its greatest achievement is making history, or at least the telling of it, conform to certain nineteenth century linguistic theories. The basic idea is that the Aryan civilization and language are not native to India. According to them, these Aryans who were nomadic barbarians from Central Asia invaded India from the northwest around 1500 BC. North India was then home to a civilization of Dravidians who were defeated and driven south—nearly a thousand miles—by the invading Aryans. These Dravidians were once thought to be a separate race, so the result was racial conflict. Such racial theories are no longer respectable, so they are now simply a distinct language group. The Aryans then composed their great literary works beginning with the Rig Veda in 1200 BC. The evidence for all of this is said to be linguistic, obtained by a linguistic and literary analysis of the Vedas. A consequence of this is — and this is inescapable—the Harappan Civilization and its language must be Dravidian. So anyone accepting the Aryan invasion and dates like 1500 BC and 1200 BC has no choice but to accept that the Vedas and Sanskrit are post Harappan. But more basically, the theories of nineteenth century linguists give us a historical scenario that asks us to reject every trace of Indian tradition over the past two thousand years and more. In effect, the Indo-European school has replaced, or attempted to replace, nearly all Indian tradition with their linguistically derived historical scenarios. Of course, I do not have to emphasize that what the Indo-Euroepan school has created is the theory of the Indo-European origin of Indian history and civilization via the Aryan invasion.

Those of us belonging to the Indo-American school approach history differently. We do not necessarily reject all tradition. We feel that a long-standing tradition must have some basis and should be accepted unless inherently implausible. This is an idea of S.B. Roy—a pioneer in chronological studies—and will illustrate this with a couple of examples. When tradition says that Arjuna married the sister of Krishna we accept it unless it can be proven otherwise. When tradition says that Yajnavalkya was Vaishampayana's sister's son, who rebelled against his teachers and went on to study in the Surya sampradaya school of Janaka, we see no reason to disbelieve it. On the other hand when tradition claims that Ravana had ten heads and twenty arms we demand irrefutable proof !

But most importantly, we do not allow linguistics the same primacy as the final arbiter on history as the Indo-European school. Also, we feel that linguistically derived models must withstand critical scrutiny, the same critical scrutiny that was supposedly applied to traditional accounts. We feel that the work of linguists has escaped such scrutiny for reasons that have nothing to do with scholarship, but as a result of political and cultural factors. Also, we feel that models of history, including linguistically derived models, must be modified or even discarded when they are contradicted by new evidence. A particular example I would like to cite is evidence from archaeology that did not exist a century ago.

Further, we believe that resources of modern science and technology must be taken advantage of in the study of history. I hpoe these points will get illustrated during the course of my presentation. And as I noted we now have a critical mass of scholars in the West—mainly in the United States and Canada—who subscribe to this approach. We are even setting up a new center called the International Institute of Indian Studies based in Ottawa, Canada, with its own flagship publication the *International Journal of Indian Studies*. It is bringing out a special issue on the Indo-Aryan Problem, and my talk in a way is a brief summary of my article "Language, Mathematics and Astronomy: A Chronological Synthesis for Vedic Age", to appear in that issue. Having laid this groundwork, let me begin my presentation proper.

Linguistic Model Of History: A Critical Examination

Let me very quickly review the basis for the current linguistically derived version of history. It is entirely a ninenteenth century European creation. It has absolutely no support in Indian tradition. It is barely two hundred years old and can be traced to the desire of Europeans to free themselves from the heritage of Jewish history and tradition. The Bible has two books, of which the Old Testament gives the traditional version of the history of the human race. It is of course a Jewish creation. To give themselves a separate identity, the Christian Europe looked East. They had two choices—India and China. To them the Indian Aryans were preferable as ancestors to the Chinese. So they became the Aryans. This idea seemed to have receive scientific support when Sir William Jones identified Sanskrit as a relative of European languages like Latin and Greek. Of course Sanskrit is related to other languages like Kannada, Telugu and Tamil, and also to Southeast Asian languages like Malay, Thai and Indonesian, but that had no sponsors. A combination of historical and sociological factors exaggerated the Indo-European connection and the "Aryan race" out of all proportion. So it should not come as a surprise that the word Aryan was grotesquely perverted by the Nazis and Hilter in this century.

By this I do not want to suggest that all scholars propounding the Aryan origin of India were anti-Semites and racists to the same degree. Far from it! Men like Max Müller would not be caught dead with such people! Also several distinguished Indologists like Jacobi and Goldstücker were themselves Jewish. Nevertheless, in studying the works of nineteenth century scholars it would be extremely naive not to recognize that they were working in a climate quite different from our own. It simply cannot be taken as objective scholarship. Many of them, perhaps a majority, were missionaries and government servants whose training and education, not to say outlook, were extremely narrow. It was considered entirely proper and even patriotic to color history to meet political needs, as was done in this century in Communist Russia and China. Then there was also the issue of religion. The prestigious

Boden Chair of Sankrit at Oxford University was endowed by Colonel Boden in 1811 specifically to promote Sanskrit learning among the English, so as 'to enable his countrymen to proceed in the conversion of the natives of India to the Christian Religion.'

Even prizes were offered to literary works undermining Indian tradition. The first occupant of the Boden Chair was Horace Hyman Wilson. Writing about a series of lectures he gave, Wilson himself noted:

These lectures were written to help candidates for a prize of 200 pounds given by John Muir...for the best refutation of the Hindu religious systems.

I am happy to report that the Boden Professor of Sanskrit at Oxford no longer indulges in such unseemly activities! Its occupants in recent times have been some of the most distinguished scholars in the world. I mention these facts only to point out that we cannot accept the claims and views of nineteenth century scholars at their face value. Even such eminent scholars as Max Müller were not free from such equivocal standards as his letters clearly show. These scholars were often driven by more than a simple search for knowledge. The objectivity of these scholars was simply not up to present day standards. Of course we would be wrong to apply today's standards to an earlier age, but we would be no less wrong to accept their conclusions without examining all sides. So let us accept once and for all that these men and women were products of the age in which they lived, and were as much a part of the social and cultural milieu—with its values, prejudices and beliefs—as the people and the politicians that gave rise to them. The same is true of us. A century from now most of us will probably cut a sorry figure, and some of us may not have to wait that long. In this regard they were probably no different from an orthodox Brahmin who may be a great scholar, but bigoted in his attitude towards other castes. With this background, let us begin to focus on the technical aspects of nineteenth century linguistics, which is really our main interest.

When a historian today cites "linguistic evidence" for the date of the Aryan invasion, the Aryan-Dravidian conflict, or the date of composition of the Rig Veda, he is really-citing one opinion among many. There is no firm evidence for any of them. It was max Müller who proposed 1200 BC as the date for the Rig Veda on virtually no evidence at all. It was his immense prestige more than anything else that made it widely accepted. But even today there is no consensus about these dates, or even for the invasion. Here are a sampling of opinions of some well known scholars.

The Rig Vedic hymns were composed over a period of from about 1500 BC to 100 BC, with some hymns of a later period. The other three Vedas are dated to approximately 800 to 500 BC... Romila Thapar (1992)...

Many commentators have concluded that some of these passages [from the Rig Veda] refer to the initial conquests of the land by heroic, nomadic tribesmen, the Arya. But this interpretation assumes that the Arya, to whom the hymns refer, were intrusive to north India or Pakistan, and there is nothing in the Vedic hymns themselves which made such a conclusion necessary. Colin Renfrew (1988)

The homeland, the race and the culture of a supposed Proto-Indo-European population has been discussed, a population which may possibly never have existed. N.S. Trubitskoy (1934)

.... central and eastern Anatolia was the key area where an early form of Proto-Indo-European was spoken before 6500 BC. Colin Renfrew (1988)

Whether the Vedic hymns were composed in 1000, 1500 or 2000 or 3000 BC, no power on earth will ever determine. F. Max Müller (c.1865)

So we have a choice from 1000 BC to 6500 BC for the Aryans, with Max Müller himself giving us a choice from 1000 BC to 3000 BC. How he came up with 1200 BC is an interesting stroy by itself. His sole evidence was a ghost story written by Somadeva in about AD 1100, more than 2000 years after the supposed invasion! It is a fact of life that those citing linguistic evidence are in reality basing it on a ghost story.

The next question then is does the nineteenth century linguistics stand as a science upon which we can base important conclusions? For an answer will quote the view of Frits Staal, one of the world's foremost linguists today:

We can now assert, with the power of hindsight, that

Indian linguists in the fifth century B.C.E. knew and understood more than Western linguists in the nineteenth century AD. Can one not extend this conclusion and claim that it is probable that Indian linguists are still ahead of their Western colleagues and may continue to be so in the next century?

When Professor Staall says Indian linguists, he means those following the traditional line of Indian scholarship, and not modern college professors who more or less follow Western fashions. Thus nineteenth century linguists like Max Müller were 2500 years behind such linguists as Panini and Patanjali! This view is confirmed by modern computer scientists working in Artificial Intelligence who are discovering new applications for such ancient works, while finding 'modern' linguistics almost totally useless—a fact that I can attest to from personal experience as one who has worked in the field of Artificial Intelligence for more than ten years. At American universities, linguists and computer scientists are rediscovering the mathematical rigor found in such masterpieces as Panini's *Ashtadhyayi* and Pantanjali's *Mahabhasya*. In fact, I do not think I would be far wrong to say that the only scholars still interested in nineteenth century philology are Indologists! It is of course beyond question that European scholarship has made an enormous contribution to the progress of modern India, not only in science and technology but also in the legal, political and social fields. The Indian renaissance in the nineteenth century would be unthinkable without the European impulse. No one can deny that. But linguistics was really a great leap backwards. And we have now come a full circle because as I just told you American linguistics and computer scientists have begun a serious study of Panini and other ancient Indian linguists.

And no Indian linguist has ever classified languages into Aryan and Dravidian families or tried to connect it to historical people or races. Aryan denotes a culture. Dravidian, a relatively late term, refers to a geographical region that also includes Maharashtra and Gujarat. This classification of languages is an extremely superficial method compared to the profound analysis of language and phonology found in works like Panini's *Ashtadhyayi.*

Summarizing the situation, I will say that neither on technical grounds, nor on the ground of objectivity can linguistic theories be allowed to enjoy any special position above and beyond all other approaches. Further, the record so far shows that the results of these methods are too subjective and imprecise. Also, it is frequently contradicted by archaeological and other data. As will point out, its chronology frequently leads to errors exceeding 2000 years. This more than anything has caused us to give up relying on nineteenth century linguistics as a tool in historical research. But the main thing is not that the work of these nineteenth century scholars is not intersting, but simply it is unequal to the task before us. The same can be said for nearly all the work that is more than a hundred years old—in medicine and engineering for example. Nineteenth century philology is no exception. It is a relic from the past. Like alchemy, it is an approach and a method that failed. It happens all the time in science. It is one of the occupational hazards of research.

Harappan Civilization And The Rig Veda

As indicated previously, accepting the Aryan invasion theory of Max Müller and his chronology irrevocably places the composition of the Rig Veda after the end of the Harappan civilization. Note that the so-called Harappan civilization, also called the Indus Valley civilization has been seriously misconstrued. The first two cities found happened to be Harappa on the Ravi and Mohenjo-Daro on the Indus. But we now know, which scholars did not seventy years ago, that they are part of more than 2500 settlements stretching from Baluchistan to the Ganga and beyond and down to the Tapti valley, covering nearly a million and a half square kilometres. Also, most of these settlements are concentrated not along the Indus or even the Ganga, but along the now dry Saraswati river. The map I have given, though a little out of date, gives an idea of the distribution of the so-called 'Indus' sites, except that most of them are not along the Indus at all. This distribution is confirmed by the Rig Veda. The Rig Veda celebrates not the Ganga but the Saraswati as the holiest of rivers. The Ganga is mentioned only once while the Saraswati is lauded thirty times at least. Thus the Rig Veda and archaeology are in agreement. So whatever the Rig Veda may or may not say, it most emphatically describes North India as it was before the Saraswati dried up. That is to say the Rig Veda is pre-Harappan.

The question next is when did the Saraswati dry up? This we can pinpoint quite accurately. Extensive hydrological surveys by V.S. Wakankar and his team, as well as the work of the other Indian and American archaeologists establishes that the Saraswati changed its course several times and went dry around 1900 BC. The cause of this was the loss of two of its major tributaries—the Sutlej and the Yamuna—the first to the Indus and the other to the Ganga. Satellite photographs also confirm that the Saraswati was once a mighty river, nearly eight kilometres wide in places. This is essentially what the Rig Veda also tells us. This calamity—the drying up of the Saraswati—and not any invasion was what led to the disruption and abandonment of the so-called Indus civilization, which really should be called the Saraswati civilization.

This immediately leads us to a couple of anomalous situations to say the least. First, if the Aryans came into India only about 1500 BC and composed the Rig Veda around 1200 BC, how did they describe a river and geography as it was before 1900 BC ? Even more puzzling, why did they cross six great rivers—the Indus and its five tributaries—only to set up a great civilization, and worship it as the holiest of rivers? The verdict of archaeology therefore is clear and unambiguous: the Rig Veda describes North India as it was before the decline of the Harappan culture. Therefore, the Harappan society was Vedic Aryan. And the Aryan Dravidian divide is modern day fiction.

Linguists have implicitly assumed that the geography has always been the same. But we now know this is not the case at all. Since the ending of the last Ice Age around 8000 BC, North India has undergone cataclysmic, tectonic and hydrological upheavals. The Saraswati changed its course at least three time before going completely dry around 1900 BC. Also, not only the Sutlej and the Yamuna, but at one time even the Ganga used to flow into the Saraswati. So we must go back and reexamine our ancient works for any possible hints about these cataclysms. For instance, the legend of Bhagiratha bringing the Ganges may refer to one of these changes of the river courses. The same may be said about the story of Kuru Samvarana.

I will later show, or at least try to show that the high Harappan culture—c. 3000 to 1900 BC—is post-Rig Vedic, in a manner to be made specific. It represents in fact the age of the Sutras, the Brahmanas and the Upanishads. This I propose to show by a comparison of the Sutras with Old-Babylonia (1700 BC) and ancient Egypt. But first another dramatic piece of evidence from the Vedic Age.

I have here a photograph of a Vedic Aryan bronze head found near Delhi by the American collector Harry Hicks in 1958. He barely saved it from being melted down for scrap, and we should all be eternally grateful to Harry for preserving this priceless object from our past. He and the American physicist Robert Anderson subjected it to a series of tests in scientific laboratories in America and Switzerland in an effort to determine its date. To their great surprise it was found to have been cast around 3700 BC! Even more remarkably, the Head fits very closely to the description of the famous sage Vasishta given in the *danastutis* of the seventh mandala and a contemporary of Viswamitra who is the seer of the third mandala. The two were present as advisors of the Bharata King Sudas when he defeated a coalition of ten princes in what is known as the Battle of Ten Kings. Hicks and Anderson date this battle to 3730 BC. I can arrive at roughly the same date from completely different considerations, as we shall soon see. This battle, as the great American Vedic Scholar David Frawley has noted, marked the end of an era, just like the later Mahabharata War. The Battle of Ten Kings ended the Rig Vedic Age, while the Mahabharata War ended the Vedic Age proper, with the final editing of the four Vedas by Vyasa and his school.

Also note that the identification of the Head as a likeness of Vasishta is secondary, though evidence strongly points to it. The very existence of a Head described by the Rig Veda cast nearly 6000 years ago is sufficient to demolish the theory and the chronology of the Aryan invasion. Incidentally, this archaeologically derived date is supported by tradition. According to the "King's list", from Sudas to Abhimanyu is sbout 630 years. If we accept (for the present) the traditional date of 3102 BC for the Mahabharata War, we arrive at c. 3730 BC for Sudas and his contemporary Vasishta. Also Brihadbala of Kosala who was thirty-first in descent from Rama, son of Dasharatha, was killed by Abhimanyu at Kurukshetra. Taking twenty years per generation which is known to be a good average when long dynasties are involved, we get between 3800 and 3700 BC for Rama, and therefore also for Vasishta who was his senior contemporary.

There is other archaeological evidence. The so-called

Harappan sites from Baluchistan to Gujarat show Vedic sacrificial altars. So the inhabitants of these settlements followed Vedic ritual, in fact the most important of them. It is therefore not surprising that historians of the Aryan migration school fight shy of archaeology, some going so far as to claim that archaeology is irrelevant! A well known historian whom I do not wish to name wrote recently telling us.

There is therefore little point in turning to archaeology for evidence of the 'the Aryans', yet attempts are made to do this.

I think it is a rather sad sight to see historians reduced to making such statements in the hopes of preserving a crumbling theory. I can fully sympathize with their position. It cannot be a pleasant feeling to find oneself on a sinking ship. But trying to preserve a lost paradigm by denying all evidence will at best prolong the agony.

In this you will have observed that I have used the traditional date of 3102 BC for the Mahabharata War. If you had asked me a year ago I would have said 1425 BC. In fact I tried very hard to prove that date— both by astronomy and by other means. But the evidence of astronomy overwhelmingly supports the traditional date. Even the one astronomical statement in the Mahabharata, if the time of Bhishma's death, after careful reading, I am able to show points to circa 3000 BC as the date, and not 1300 or 1400 BC as claimed by some. But what really settled the issue of the date for me was the flow of ancient mathematics from India to Egypt and Old-Babylonia. This work which is based on the pioneering research of the American mathematician and historian of science A. Seidenberg opens a totally new approach to the study of ancient chronology. And this approach, as much as any other, distinguishes what I have called the Indo-American school. This mathematical evidence gives a lower limit of 2000 BC for the early Sutra literature, that can later be pushed to 2700 BC based on comparisons with the Third Dynasty of Egypt of 2650 BC. And this is what I want to talk about next.

The Sulbasutras And The Trail Of Ancient Mathematics

Thanks to recent research, we now know that the trail of mathematical knowledge is quite different from what is usually found in history books. A majority of historians still believe that Old-Babylonian and Egyptian mathematics predates the Indian. But this view is no longer tenable. Seidenberg has established that the mathematics of both Pythagorean Greece and Old-Babylonia of 1700 BC as well as of the Egyptian Middle Kngdom of 2000 to 1800 BC are derivatives of the Baudhayana Sulba. In the Baudhauana Sulba we find both the origination and the development of the so-called 'Theorem of Pythagoras', probably the most important theorem in geometry. But first let me spend a little time talking about the Sutra literature and particularly the Sulbas.

After the closing of the Vedic period, this is to say when the Vedas were classified and turned into a closed canon, a systematic effort was mounted to codify the knowledge and the ritual of the Vedas in the form of principles that could be easily memorized. The Vedas were already becoming unintelligible, and so a need was felt for such an effort. An extremely important part of the Sutra literature was what was called the Kalpasutras which lay down the rules or guidelines for basic household and other duties as well as for rituals. The rituals or the Srauta part contains the famous Sulbasutras which are mathematical texts which give in great detail the mathematical details necessary for the construction of Vedic altars for various kinds of rituals and sacrfices. And it is in connection with these ritualistic needs that the earliest mathematics evolved.

The Sulbasutras, or the Sulbas, have attracted a lot of attention, but for the most part, the scholars who first examined them—mainly philologists—were mathematically ill equipped to make a proper study of it. Also, since the Aryan invasion model as well Max Müller's chronology had by then become established, the Sulbas along with their authors were dated absurdly late—as late as 250 BC by Keith. A result of this was that some European scholars and their Indian followers have continued to insist that the Sulbas are copies of Greek mathematics following the invasion of Alexander! Others however claim that both Indian and Greek mathematics are derived from Babylonia. This was the result of ignorance and prejudice, to somehow derive everything from Greece. Before I go into details, it is worth noting that the very existence of elaborately planned cities like Harappa, Mohenjo-Daro, Lothal and others is evidence of condiderable knowledge of geometry and mathematics. They could not possibly have used mathematics from Pythagorean or Alexandrian Greece!

This is further strengthened by the existence of Vedic altars described in the Sulbas. In summary, I have to say that the Greek influence on India has been exaggerated out of all proportion to reality. It was nothing but a nineteenth century European fantasy.

When we compare the Sulbas to Old-Babylonian mathematics, the trail of mathematical flow unmistakably is from the Sulbas to Old-Babylonia. Workers before Seidenberg's monmental study stated it otherwise, but that was due largely to haste and unfamiliarity. His findings are now being woven into modern works and it is only a matter of time before they make their way universally. Previously, historians of science had been persuaded by Sanskrit scholars that the trail had to be from Babylonia to India because the Aryans could not have been in India before 1500 BC! Seidenberg was quite emphatic when he observed:

Hence we do not hesitate to place the Vedic altar rituals, or, more exactly, rituals exactly like them, far back of 1700 BC.

To Summarize the argument: the elements of ancient geometry found in Egypt and Babylonia stem from a ritual system of the kind observed in the Sulbasutras.

Note that he places the Vedic altar rituals far back of 1700 bc, and also recognizes that in the Sutras, mathematics is secondary to religion and ritual. Baudhayana derives everyone of his reullts in connection with a religious altar. In fact, in the Baudhayana Sulba we can actually see him derive the Pythagorean theorem from the caturasrasyena-cit Vedic altar. But Sanskrit scholars objected to Seidenberg's derivation since it violated their own linguistic chronology. So Seidenberg complained :

Sanskrit scholars do not give me a date so far back as 1700 bc [for the Sulbasutras]. Therefore I postulate a pre-Old-Babylonian source for the kind of geometric rituals we see preserved in the Sulbasutras, or at least for the mathematics involved in these rituals.

He was forced into this artificial argument because accepting their chronology leads to mathematical contradictions. There is no way of deriving the mathematics of the Sulba from Old-Babylonia of 1700 bc, or of the Egyptian Middle Kingdom of 2000 to 1800 bc. On the other hand, as Seidenberg noted, both Egypt and Old-Babylonia use mathematical results derived from Vedic rituals given in the Sulbas. Building on Seidenberg's work we obtain what amounts to a mathematical proof that the early Sutra literature was in existence no later than 2000 bc. This means that the earliest layer of the Sutra authors – Baudhayana, Aswalayana, Apastamba and Katyayana must be dated to no later than 2000 bc. I would not be surprised if this is the first example of a mathematical "theorem" used in history! As a consequence, the Mahabharata War must also be dated to before 2000 bc. And this fact, more than any other convinced me that a popular date of 1400 bc for the Mahabharata War is not tenable. As we shall soon see, this readily leads to the traditional date of 3102 bc or thereabouts for the event.

This suggests that there was a direct link between Egypt and India going back at least to 2000 bc. And there are several others which I do not need to go into here. I have found another, I think dramatic connection which may take us even further back, almost to 2700 bc. It is well known of course that the Egyptian pyramid is always a funerary structure. Where did the idea of using pyramid shaped structures as resting place for the dead originate? I have been able to trace it also to the Sulbas. Note that all Vedic altars except one are prismatic; that is the base and the top have exactly the same shape and size and horizontal surface. The only exception is the smasana-cit or the cemetery shaped altar. This is a pyramid. The prayer used with the *samasana-cit* is from the Taittiriya Samhita and it says:

"May we gain prosperity in the world of our fathers"

What could be plainer? We have geometric and religious connection between the India of the Sutra period and ancient Egypt! The pyramid of the Third Dynasty and earlier is a flat topped structure called the *mastaba*. It is the forerunner of the classical true pyramid of he Fourth Dynasty that we invariably associate with Egypt. I have here pictures of the *mastaba* as well as the *smasana-cit;* note that the former is the same as the latter except it is made to rest on is rectangular base instead of its trapezoidal side. (See Figure.) It grew enormously in size (which may have been the reason for its change of orientation), but the simple prayer: "May we gain prosperity in the world of our fathers" remained unchanged through millennia. Both the description of the *smasána-cit* altar and the prayer from the Taittiriya Samhita are found in the Baudhayana Sulba. And as I said there are other mathematical connections, and all of these cannot be simply a coincidence. I therefore hold it be beyond question that India of the Kalpa Sutras and Egypt of the Third Dynasty and earlier were in contact. This also shows that the Harappan Civilization was of the Sutra period. This is confirmed by astronomy, which is my next topic.

Evidence Of Vedic Astronomy

It should first be noted that because of important recent developments, especially as a result of the decipherment of an astronomical code in the Rig Veda by the Indian American cryptologist Subhash Kak, our whole perspective on ancient astronomy will have to change.And this affects not only Indian astronomy, but all of ancient astronomy. Until recently, it was believed that the Vedanga Jyotisha of Lagadha (c. 1200 BC) contained the earliest Indian astronomical knowledge. It must now be acknowledged that the Rig Veda, and possibly other works until the drying up of the Saraswati, were in some ways more advanced astronomically than the Vedanga Jyotisha which is primarily an astronomical almanac or calendar. The Rig Veda on the other hand contains remarkably accurate estimates for the orbital periods of the five major planets and also of the Sun and the Moon. So their knowledge went well beyond preparing almanacs. There are hints, but as yet no proof, that they also possessed knowledge of eclipses and their prediction. The main point is that we must take astronomical statements in the Vedic literatures seriously. This particularly applies to the pioneering work of Tilak and Jacobi going back to 1893. David Frawley's recent work on Vedic astronomy also lends support to their findings.

Figure: At the top is the *mastaba*, the forerunner of the Egyptian pyramid; at the bottom is the *smasanacit* Vedic altar described by Baudhayana. Note that the *mastaba* is essentially the *smasana-cit* turned arouund.

The first point I want to comment is that astronomy and archaeology are in agreement as regards the date of Vasishta, assuming that the Hicks-Anderson identification is correct. The Rig Veda knows the vernal equinox in Mrigashira (Orion) and none later. In fact the seventh mandala itself, which may be called the Book of Vasishta, records the Orion equinox. The next star would have been the Rohini (Aldebaran) and the Rig Veda therefore falls between 4000 BC and 3000 BC, closer perhaps to the upper limit. The Mahabharata knows the Rohini equinox, c. 3000 BC. Thus the Hicks-Anderson date of 3800- 3700 BC for Vasishta is consistent with astronomy.

Now for a small technical observation. From time immemorial Indians have followed a sidereal model of astronomy. That is they note the cardinal points of the year with reference to the fixed stars. Thus the Indian Zodiac is at least a thousand years older than the Babylonian Zodiac, and Vedic astronomy most certainly cannot be a borrowing from Babylon. There is no way the Indians could have derived data going well back before 4000 BC, using a system borrowed no later than 1700 BC. This requires knowledge of Newton's Law of Graviation and the solution of differential equations. So the astronomical observation recorded in ancient works such as the Vedas and the Brahmanas have to be taken as authentic. Fabricating data is infinitely more difficult than recording observations. An illiterate cannot be a successful forger. Linguists like Keith and Whitney who made such allegations were only exhibiting their own scientific and mathematical ignorance.

With the background it is now relatively easy to detemine the date of the early Sutra literature. We have seen that Baudhayana, Aswalayana and others belonging to the earliest layer of the Sutra period must be dated to before 2000 BC because of the Egyptian connection, based on Seidenberg's (any my own) work. I will not use my results relating to the identification of Baudhayana's work with the Egyptian Third Dynasty pyramids yet, because I feel it needs more research. But will use the data provided by Aswalayana. He notes that the plants sprout after the first rains in the month of Bhardrapada; this now takes place in Jyeshta. This indicates a shift in the seasons of at least 60 days, possibly more. Seasons fall back at the rate of one day roughly every 72.5 years. This places Asālayana before 2300 BC. Taking 70 days brings Awsalayana almost to 3000 BC. But I can make this more precise by his reference to the pole star.

The pole star that we are used to seeing now is Polaris. Its technical name is Ursa Minoris. Some of you may not know that there has not been a pole star, that is to say, a stationary star making the north pole through much of human history. For instance there was no pole star at the time of Jesus Christ. This is because the axis of the earth falls back very slowly relative to the fixed stars, the same phenomenon that causes the seasons to fall back. So the presence of a pole star is a relatively rare phenomenon in history. The pole star observed by Aswalyana can only have been the star Alpha Draconis, also known as Thuban found in the constellation of the Dragon. This places him no later than 2500 BC, and no earlier than say 3000 . The pole star is not known to the Rig Veda, but the Shatapatha Brahmana knows it. There is other astronomical evidence also that place both Aswalayana and the Shatapatha Brahmana around 2950 BC when the Krittikas (Pleiades) touched the ecliptic in the east at the time of the vernal equinox, when the equinox moved from Rohini to Krittika. The Fourth Dynasty of Egypt of course is famous for its pyramids.

It should be noted that they also note the pole star Thuban from about 2600 BC onwards. Thus astronomy also connects ancient Egypt and India of the Sutra period. They both observed the same pole star! We earlier saw that mathematics and religious practice also make ancient Egypt and India of the Sutra period contemporary. There is no way all of this can be sheer coincidence. The odds against it are astronomical.

I will next turn to the Mahabarata War. It cannot be later than Aswalayana for he mentions it. So the Mahabharata War must be placed before 2500 BC. Tradition places Aswalayana five teaching generations from Krishna of the Mahabharata. Thus the traditional date of Mahabharata— 3102 BC— is fully in agreement with *c.* 2900 BC for Aswalayana. Tradition also gives him about the same data (3000 BC). This agrees with astronomy and also with the Egyptian and other connections. I have found it is also in agreement with the earliest Chinese chronology which begins with the Krittika (Pleides) vernal equinox observed in 2680 BC. will not go into that subject here.

So I find support for the traditional date for the Mahabharata War from two independent sources: first, literary archaeological; and second, the comparison of ancient mathematics from Egypt and the Sulbas. I cannot overemphasize the importance of this cross-cultural connection. The pyramids and Egyptian mathematics are there, and there is no way of deriving both the mathematics and the geometric rituals of the Kalpasurtras (of which Sulba is part) from the arithmetic of Egypt.

But before I go on to give my final summary, I would like to make a few observatios on the need to reexamine the foundations of history of science, and not just history. In astronomy, as in mathematics, linguistic schloarship has exaggerated the influence of Greece upon India out of all proportion to reality. Sometimes I feel that all these scholars were ever doing was to scan Indian scientific works to locate the word *yavana*, so that they could claim Greek influence on the whole work! Incidentlly the word *yavana* does not necessarily mean Ionian as our linguist friends claim. The Mahabharata says that the *yavanas* are the descendants of Turvasu and his tribe. And Turvasu was one of the princes driven out of India by King Sudas following his victory in the Battle of Ten Kings. So we can with more justification claim that the Ionians are really descendants of the *yavanas* Turvasu and his people–following their exile. This is not as fanciful as it my seem. There is now strong evidence for the migration of Indians out of India into Iran, Mesopotamia, Syria and Anatolia shortly after 2000 BC. This is exactly what we should except following a great clamity like the drying up of a major water source like the Saraswati. But using the approach of linguists, I can even show that the YMCA youth auditorium called Yavanika across the street from here represents Greek influence. From there it is just one step more to claim that Bangalore was a Greek settlement, and its founder Kempe Gouda must have been a Greet invader. Also note that the Greeks who came to India with Alexander the Great were not Ionians; they were Macedonians.. So why should the Indians call them *yavana?*

So my main point is we must now recognize that there were two phases to ancient astronomy. The first phase was the Vedic, for which we can take 2000 BC as the closing point, corresponding roughly to the drying up of the Saraswati. Then there was a Dark Age. From what remained from this astronomy, and possibly borrowing from the later Babylonians, Lagadha compiled the Vedanga Jyotisha around 1200 BC. Note that at that time, Babylonia was ruled by Kassites, very probably a people of Indian origin who had over-thrown the Old-Babylonian empire of Hammurabi around 1720 BC. So these Babylonians, especially the ruling elite were an Indo-Aryan people. Very probably, Zarathushtra also belongs to the Kassite period. But in some ways the Vedanga Jyotisha is more narrow in outlook than the concept of a stronomy found in the Rig Veda. The 27 star Zodiac is also much older that the Vedanga Jyotisha. It goes back at least to Taittiriya Samhita.

Summary And Conclusions

A critical analysis of the Aryan invasion theory in the light of modern data and scientific methods shows it to be wholly without foundation. It was a historical accident and the outgrowth of the cultural and political climate of nineteenth century colonialism. It is based on some speculative theories of some linguists who lacked the objectivity and the scientific background necessary to carry out research in the modern sense. Their theories are also largely rejected by modern linguists. Like alchemy in the middle ages, it was a model that failed. Its main contributions—the Aryan invasion of India in the late ancient age, and the Aryan-Dravidian conflicts—are speculative theories that are contradicted by all data. Its chronology is nothing but figment of the imagination, created by appealing to a ghost story written about AD 1100. The whole edifice is little more than a historical curiosity, created by persons who by training and outlook were ill-equipped to make an objective study of an alien and ancient culture.

The Harappan culture was part of a continuing evolution that has its antecedents in India itself going back well beyond 6000 BC. The major part of the Harappan civilization excavated so far—c. 3000 to 1800 BC—I believe represents the early Sutra and the Brahmana periods. This I believe to be largely post Vedic and post Mahabharata War. This identification is based on recent findings in mathematics of the Sulbasutras and the mathematics of Egypt of 2000 BC, and secondarily Old-Babylonia of 1700 BC. This phase of the Indian civilization was brought to an end around 1900 BC by the final drying up of the Saraswati river. What followed in India was a Dark Age.

This was cataclysm of the first magnitude, though Indian society had already been weakened by geographical and political upheavals in the previous thousand years or so. This also led to a massive outlfow of people, especially of the elite, west into Iran, Mesopotamia and other neighboring regions. For the next thousand years and more dynasties and rulers with Indian names appear and disappear all over West Asia. Even as late as around 600 BC, the founder of the Median Empire in Western Iran was Uvakshatra. The actual name of the ancient Kurus. The Achaemenid empire of Persia was full of names of Indian origin, names like Dayavarsha (Darius), Kshayarsha (Xerxes), Arthakshatra (Artaxerxes), Sthidarpana (Thissaphernes) and Kambujia (Cambyses). And the governor of a province was called *kshetrapavana* which has been shortened to satrap. Once we recognize the possibility of this westward movement of the Indian Aryans, the postulated Indo-Iranian ancestors become a wholly unnecessary contrivance. The Bhavishya Purana has records that imply that Zoroaster was a fire worshipping heretic. Our history books note none of this. They begin Indian histroy with the wholly fictitious Aryan invasion and the Aryan-Dravidian conflict resulting in the destruction of the Harappan civilization.

I suggest the following chronological summary for the ancient age. It is paramount importance that Indian history be studied in conjunction with the contemporaneous neighboring societies.

1. The Rig Vedic Age ended with the battle of Ten Kings c. 3730 BC. Rama, son of Dasharatha belongs to this era. Contemporary neighboring societies—First Dynasty of Egypt; Proto-Assyrian (Asura)?
   The early Saraswati civilization: before 3700 BC.

2. The Mahabharata War: c. 3100 BC. Closing of the Vedic Age. Early disruptions in the geography and the hydrology of North India. First and Second Dynasties of Egypt; Proto-Sumerians, Proto-Assyrians.
   The middle Saraswati civilization: 3700 to 3000 BC.

3. 3000 to 1800 BC: Harappan culture. The age of Sutras and Brahmanas. Aswalayana, Baudhayana, etc. Egyptian Third and Fourth Dynasties and later. Sumerians. The Gradual decline and drying up of the Saraswati.
   The late Saraswati civilization: 3000 to 1800 BC.

4. 1800 to 900 BC? Age of chaos. Migration of Indian elite to West Asia and Mesopotamia. Founding of the Kassite, Hittite and Mittani Empires.

This is merely a chronological framework. It is to be regarded as tentative following the collapse of the Aryan invasion theory and the Indo-European version of history.

But the idea of Indian history begining with the Aryan invasion and the Aryan-Dravidian divide is wholly a fiction. Our future studies in histroy, which really means rebuilding ancient history from scratch, has to use scientific methods, archaeological and all other evidence, AND INDIAN TRADITION. I hope I have made my point—the need for a new approach, one that I have called Indo-American. But that is just a name. My main point is the following: throwing away everything and building a scenario based on some antiquated linguistic theories and calling it history doesn't make it history. It makes myth and fiction.

BIBLIOGRAPHY

1. David Frawely 1991, *Gods, Sages and Kings,* Passage Press, Salt Lake City, Utah. Indian Edition, Motilal-Banarasidass.
2. N.S. Rajaram; Languages, Mathematics and Astronomy: A Chronological Synthesis for the Vedic Age, To apperat in the *International Journal for Indian Studies,* Special Issue on the Indo-Aryan Problem, 1994.
3. A. Seidenberg, The Origin of Mathematics, *Archive for History of Exact Science,* 18, 1978.
4. Subhash Kak, Planetary Periods from the Rig Vedic Code, *Mankind Quarterly,* 1993.
5. Subhash Kak, Archaeology and Literature: The Myth of the Aryan Invasion, To appear.

The Iron Age in India: the Beginning and Consequences

DILIP K. CHAKRABARTI* AND NAYANJOT LAHIRI**

I. Introduction

This paper is a brief statement of the current state of research on the Indian Iron Age, which in some sense updates the first author's assessment published in 1992[1].

But first, how do we define and bracket this "Age" in the Indian context? We define the Indian Iron age as the period between the significant appearance of iron in the archaeological sequence of a given area and the beginning of the early historical period in that area. The problems in bracketing this Age are more complex. Since the protohistoric background of Iron bearing horizons is pluralistic, the transitions from primarily copper -using cultures to Iron using ones and their subsequent transfigurations into the historical limelight also proceed unevenly. To take up the terminal point of this phase, the dates of the beginning of the early historic period or the phase of transition from protohistory to history are different in different parts of the country. In some parts of the Gangetic valley it is as early as c. 700 BC (cf. the date of the Northern Black Polished Ware or the NPBW at Sringaverapur)and almost certainly c. 600 BC for the valley as a whole (except its deltaic section), the northwestern border region in modern Pakistan or the area of Achaemenid occupation, and Malwa in central India. In south India, however, the historical kingdoms do not get sharply focussed till the early centuries AD. In fact, there is not much firm evidence of the transition from protohistory to history in south India and a number of other areas such as Gujarat, Bengal, Sind and Assam till the third-second centuries BC. In some sections of the Chhotanagpur plateau in Bihar (cf. Palamau and large parts of the Santhal Parganas) this continuance of 'protohistory' is possibly upto the medieval period. Thus, it is an uneven chronological line which separates protohistory from early history in India. At the other end of this "Age", we have the problem of determining the beginning of the use of iron in different areas. The answer - as we shall find later - is more or less straightforward: by c. 1000 BC virtually the whole of the subcontinent came to possess a close familiarity with the use of iron, and in certain areas the process began much earlier. We thus do not get an even chronological line here too, but for a landmass of the subcontinent's size and physiographical diversity, a multilineal course of cultural development is a natural situation.

II. Distribution of Iron Ores

The wide distribution of iron ores in the Indian subcontinent is evident from Chart I. Our purpose in outlining this distribution is to underline an elementary aspect of iron ore procurement, since iron is present almost everywhere, with the exception of the major alluvial stretches; the raw material requirements of the various iron age horizons of early India were locally sustainable. Even the minerally poor Gangetic alluvium could easily access iron from the hilly outliers which fringe these plains–the Aravallis, the Kaimur plateau, and the Chhotanagpur alignment. Equally significant is the presence of preindustrial smelting tradi-

* Faculty of Oriental Studies, University of of Cambridge
**Dept. of History, Delhi University

tions in most areas where such ore for smelting is available (Figure 1). On the analogy of indigenous ironworkers who were obtaining good quality iron in the 19th as also in the present century not only from the large and well known deposits but also from ferruginous laterite and quartz-iron -ore schist (see Chart 1), it can be argued that early iron age communities were likely to have also used a wide variety of ore bodies, and not merely such deposits which are considered to be presently commercially viable. The sheer diversity of preindustrial smelting traditions also underlines the fact that the transition to the use of iron could take place, quite independently of each other, in a number of regions of India.

III. Chalcolithic Roots of Iron Technology

The possibility of iron being a byproduct of copper technology was demonstrated theoretically and archaeologically by S. R. B. Cooke and S. Aschenbrenner in 1975.[2a] At the theoretical level, Cooke and Aschenbrenner noted that in the pyrometallurgical extraction of copper, with a large proportion of charcoal in the furnace and an ample supply of air, together with a charge containing more haematite than necessary to be reduced to ferrous oxide (which reacts with the siliceous gangue to give the fayalite slags so typical of early copper smelting) some metallic iron could be produced. More importantly, the paper pointed out the archaeologically documented presence of metallic iron in copper / bronze objects and related artefacts of the pre-iron age period at Timna (Israel), Bir Nasb (Sinai), Nichoria (Greece) and Servia (Greek Macedonia)- while generally in ancient copper and bronze objects iron was substantially less than 1%, these artefacts contained a high iron content ranging from anything between 5 to 15%. There have been subsequent writings on this theme as well and generally suggest that at the level of regional histories of iron working this idea has been widely accepted.[2b]

In India the probability of metallic iron being produced in the Copper Age itself was first put forward by M.D.N. Sahi in 1980.[3]

The iron rich slag samples from chalcolithic Ahar (Rajasthan), on the basis of which Sahi based his argument are cited below (Chart 2). More recently, iron objects and copper based artefacts with an iron content ranging from 2% to 66% have been noticed by the second author of this paper. These objects are cited below and belong to Harappan and neolithic-chalcolithic cultural contexts that are contemporary with it or belong to the period immediately postdating the mature phase of the Indus civilization (1500 BC at the latest). Taken together, the evidence clinches Sahi's observations on Ahar and forcefully suggests that the technological base for the production of iron was present in some parts of the Indian subcontinent in chalcolithic phase itself.[4]

Chart 2 :CHALCOLITHIC OBJECTS WITH OVER 2% IRON CONTENT

Sl'. No.	Site	Object	Fe (Iron)	Reference
1.	Mohenjodaro	DK 9549	4.1	MacKay 1938:481
2.	Mohenjodaro	DK 9555	2.2	McKay 1938:481
3.	Lothal	lump	4.02	Rao 1985:656
4.	Lothal	silver object	3.29	Rao 1985:656
5.	Lothal	lump	39.1	Rao 1985:658
6.	Lothal	object	66.1	Rao 1985:658
7.	Ahar	axe	6.48	Sankalia et al 1969:227
8.	Ahar	slag	45.32	Sankalia et al 1969:226
9.	Ahar	slag	48.26	Sankalia et al 1969:226

10.	Ahar	slag	43.89	Sankalia et al 1969:226
11.	Hansi	axe	23.6	Yule 1989:262
12.	Rewari	axe	32.9	Yule 1989:262
13.	Rewari	axe	8.4	Yule 1989:262
14.	Bhiwani	axe	25.8	Yule 1989:262
15.	Bhiwani	axe	20.6	Yule 1989:262
16.	Somnath	axe	2.57	Yule 1985:100

* All objects, with exception of No. 4, are copper based.

The chronological parameters of these iron and iron-rich artefacts may be briefly discussed. We will begin with the Harappan sites. Mohenjodaro and Lothal are important Harappan centres and apart from yielding copper artefacts with significant concentrations of iron, one of the objects at Lothal (No. 5) seems to be an iron object. Another Harappan site with iron objects is Allahadino in Sind, where as early as 1973, Fairservis noted the presence of iron[4]:

"Most interesting were the occasional finds of iron (pins, bands, amorphous fragments) which at first we regarded as due to later intrusions but in view of some of the contexts involved were possibly of Harappan vintage."

The occupation layers at Allahadino are of the mature urban phase and as Fairservis acknowledged, the above mentioned occurrences were of Harappan provenance. This, incidentally, also conforms to Shaffer's findings of iron artefacts and nodules in the 'Bronze Age' contexts at Mundigak, Deh Morasi Ghundai and Said Qala Tepe in south Afghanistan as well [5].

Outside the Harappan orbit, there is Ahar, where the earliest presence of iron could be contemporary with the Harappan phase and as we will subsequently demonstrate, this metallurgical centre seems to have been using iron more widely than would be suggested by the 'chalcolithic' connotation that is usually given to Period I there. It is possible that Ahar iron is not an isolated occurrence even in the context of the Rajasthan chalcolithic.A. Ghosh[6] noted that the Ochre Coloured Ware of the Ganeshwar-Jodhpura complex at Noh (Bharatpur)" is said to have produced iron as well, though details are not available" The artefacts from Hansi, Bhiwani and Rewari whose elemental compositions are mentioned in Chart 2 belong to the axe category of the amorphous Copper hoards of the south Haryana-north Rajasthan axis. In Yule's [7] classificatory scheme, they constitute the following types: Axe I (Hansi - No. 11 1 these numbers refer to the serialization of Chart 2 in the present paper ; Somnath No. 16; this is a stratified find from the post-Harappan context), Axe IIIa (Rewari- No. 12), Axe IVb (Bhiwani-No. 14), Axe IVc (Rewari-No. 13) and a miscellaneous axe (Bhiwani-No. 15). As we have argued elsewhere [8], the northern Rajasthan - southern Haryana centre of metallurgy was also contemporary with the late Harappan situation, and at least two of the abovementioned axe types can be dated on the basis of similar types found elsewhere in secure stratigraphic contexts— Hansi No. 11 is of the same type that is found at Lothal in the Harappan/late Harappan level and Somnath in the post-Harappan phase [9] while Rewari No. 12 belongs to the same type as the stratified Mitathal IIb or Late Harappan axe [10] Taken together, these objects unequivocally underline the point that the first distinct chronological phase in the development of a technology capable of producing metallic iron in the subcontinent coincides with early chalcolithic horizons.

On our part, we are not at all surprised by the existence of technological know-how relating to iron in various sites which have mature Harappan and late Harappan affinities. In the early phase of metallurgy in the Indian subcontinent, practically every type of metal was experimented with at different Harappan centres. The second author's review of the alloying traditions of early India has clearly under lined the singular importance of the Indus Civilization from this point of view [11]

"every type of binary subsequently found in the historical record is present in the metalworking tradition of that civilization, including deliberate alloying in zinc; the copper-zinc objects in Gujarat, where the concentration of zinc in one object from Lothal (6.04%) and four artefacts from Rojdi (1.00-1.54%) constitute,in fact, the earliest evidence of zinc alloying in India. The importance of Harappan metalworking in understanding the roots of later patterns of alloying is also evident in the extensive presence of mixed compositions mainly ternary alloys (copper-lead-arsenic, copper-tin-lead, copper-tin-arsenic, copper-lead-nickel, copper-tin-nickel)..... This diversity exists at the micro-level as well; at most of the Indus Civilization sites there is a variety in the range of copper based alloys, and such heterogeneity is present at major cities and at the smaller centres.....".

The point is that Harappan metalsmiths were adept at producing a wide range of copper based objects at major and minor centres. Even a site like Allahadino which is unprepossessing, relatively speaking, in its spatial dimensions (population would be approximately 80 persons), is known to have yielded 1000 metal objects as also evidence of local manufacture. That such a metallurgical site has provided iron in its excavated layers is quite logical since its metal craftspersons had an intimate familiarity with a variety of smelting and production techniques. Vincent Piggot's [12] conclusion on 'The Iron Age in Western Iran' is similar:"It is not too much to suppose that the indigenous populations were already familiar with iron, for it is becoming increasingly apparent that Bronze Age metalsmiths throughout the ancient world had experience with iron....We must assume that this could have happened with increasing regularity to Bronze Age metalsmiths, to the point that the knowledge of how to extract iron was available but only rarely exercised."

Iron was a metal which was known and understood in the Copper-Bronze Age itself. It came to be more commonly used over time. The various contexts in the different cultural zones of India in which iron acquired a more significant archaeological presence may now be discussed.

IV. The Early Iron-using areas

IV.1 North-West

KASHMIR

The existence of megaliths in the Kashmir Valley has long been known[13] but their chronology and cultural features, specially their representing the first iron-bearing horizons of that zone, have come into proper focus only after A.K. Sharma's excavations at Gufkral in 1981-82. The Gufkral sequence begins with an aceramic neolithic level which, on the basis of an uncalibrated date-range of 2420-2000 BC, dates from the early part of the third millennium. The succeeding neolithic level has two phases - early and late - coming down to the middle of the second millennium BC. The custom of erecting menhirs was introduced in the settlement after this along with rice and millet, and apparently a new type of wheelmade dull red pottery. The ceramic shapes included jars with shapeless rims, long-necked jars, bowls, basins, dishes-on-stand, medium sized globular jars and channel spouted vessels (bowls?). Three uncalibrated radiocarbon dates (BS-431, BS-433, BS-434) are said to range between 1550 and 1100 BC. Two needles and one nail (?) have been said to be the identifiable objects of iron in this level. The possibility is that most of the earlier neolithic sites have megalithic level. although such sites may not always have the direct evidence of menhirs.

BALUCHISTAN

Pirak is the only site associated with the early beginning of iron in Baluchistan [14] Situated on the Kacchi plain, this site contains as many as 11 occupational levels. Iron appears in level 6 in a limited quantity. Its use increase in levels 4 and 3. Several two-winged arrowheads have been found, one in association with a blacksmiths's furnace. There is, however, substantial cultural continuity in the form of serrated stone blades, two of the three bichrome chalcolithic pottery types and drilling rasps of copper/ bronze. The new ceramic element is a grey or black pottery, wheelmade and often burnished. There seems to have been an increased level of craft activities in level 3 denoted by fireplaces, ovens and related artefacts, although in the pre-Iron Age levels as well crucibles have been found.. Other antiquites include antler bone points often with an incised circlet on each side, beads decorated with zigzags and circles and terracotta seals with compartmented designs. The calibrated date for the iron-bearing horizons at Pirak hovers around 800 + BC.

GANDHARA GRAVE CULTURE

The distribution of this culture is in the North West

Frontier highlands and lowlands. It is not that the protohistoric occupation of the Swat valley and its adjacent area begins only with this grave complex and Period I at Ghaligai goes back, in fact, to 3000 BC. The Grave Culture in Statcul's classification [15] belongs to Period V of the Ghaligai sequence. Two phases of this culture are neolithic-chalcolithic, iron only appearing in Period VII or the third and last phase of the complex. Apart from the appearance of iron, it is not particularly easy to isolate features which may be said to be confined only to this period, either in pottery forms and style or in usage of raw materials. The burials seem to have been fractional but the method of cremation was not entirely unknown. In some cases the graves contained burials of two periods, the bones deposited earlier being swept aside to make room for the new deposit. The associated pottery includes a grey ware of different shades and red and brown wares. The grave goods, include those of copper, gold, silver, glass, bone, terracotta spindle whorls or beads and terracotta human figurines. At a number of excavated graves iron is limited but in the total range of iron tools are the spearhead, arrowhead, pin/nail, spoon, finger ring, and cheek bar. A date of around 1000 BC has been suggested for this culture.

IV.2 West India (Southeast Rajasthan and Gujarat)

AHAR

Ahar is on the outskirts of modern Udaipur in south-east Rajasthan [16] and shows three phases of protohistoric occupation (Ahar Ia, Ib and Ic), topped by early historic levels. The credit of drawing attention to the occurrence of iron in protohistoric Ahar Ib and Ic goes to M.D.N. Sahi (1979). Ahar Ia is dated to around 2100/2000 BC (uncalibrated). The trench-wise distribution of iron artefacts at this site is as follows.

Trench	Layer	Arefact	Period	Radiocarbon date(unca.)
C	2	arrowhead	Ic	
C	2	arrowhead	Ic	
C	3	nail	Ib	1725/110 BC
D	1	arrowhead	Ic	
D	1	chisel	Ic	
D	1	peg	Ic	
D	2	socket	Ic	
E	3	ring	Ib	
L	1	chisel	Ic	
L	2	arrowhead	Ic	
X	5	arrowhead	Ic	
X	5	arrowhead	Ic	1270/100; 1550/110 BC

In Trench X, Layer 4 has been marked as a pit. However, the iron-yielding layer 5 below it is not a pit and the fact that this layer is not disturbed is further indicated by the radiocarbon sample form this layer giving the date of 1270/100 BC(uncalib.). The reported 12 iron objects from Ahar are spread in 5 trenches and in 2 phases. There cannot be any question of their being unstratified 'pit material'.

That the find of iron objects in the second and third phases of the three phase Ahar culture is not an aberration of some kind is also demonstrated by the occurrence of these iron objects in the same contexts with etched carnelian beads and one example of 'brilliant ultramarine blue' bead of lapis lazuli. These beads certainly denote the interaction of the Ahar culture with the Indus civilization. Out of the 5 reported etched carnelian beads in the protohistoric context at Ahar, four have been illustrated, although one of these illustrated specimens is from the surface. The context of three illustrated stratified examples is the following:

Figure, and No.	Trench	Layer	Period and Phase
98,6	H	2	Ib
98,7	D	3	Ib
98,9	D	1	Ic

It may be noted that Trench D, layer 1 yielded an iron object as well. The lone lapis lazuli bead occurs in Ahar Ic, its trench and layer number being C(4).

The black-and-red ware deposit (distinctly different in composition from Ahar) of Noh in the Bharatpur district is also iron bearing [17] Period I there is represented by the Ganeshwar-Jodhpura Ochre Coloured Pottery, which belongs to the major metallurgical neolithic-chalcolithic complex of northeast Rajasthan. Period II constitutes the black-and-red ware deposit and this was succeeded by Painted Grey Ware and NBP Period III. The sequence at Jodhpura in Jaipur district is also fairly similar to that of Noh [18]

LOTHAL

The occurrence of iron at Lothal has already been noted. Unfortunately, the context of these objects - like the context of all other analysed copper objects- has not been given in the report. We can tentatively put them in Lothal Period B, Phase V, i.e., the late Harappan context at Lothal. Phase VA has two radiocarbon dates: 1865/110 Bc and 1800/140 bC (both uncalibrated). They suggest the same chronological range as Ahar B.

The situation was, in fact, aptly summed up by Dr. Bijon Bihari Lal, the chief chemist of the Archaeological Survey of India [19]

"It would thus be seen that the specimen No. 15112 is made of iron.... There is no doubt that the artisans at Lothal....made use of copper, silver and iron for the manufacture of metal goods...There is no doubt that the use of gold, silver, copper, iron and bronze was fully understood."

IV.3 Central India

NAGDA

This site on the bank of the Chambal river in Malwa, excavated as early as 1955-57 [20] is still the principal site from our present point of view, because it is here that we get a clear and published stratigraphy of the early occurrence of iron in the region (Nagda Period II) and its relation both to the earlier 'Malwa chalcolithic' (Nagda Period I) and the later early historic or NBP (Nagda Period III) levels. The following facts regarding iron at this site are clear.

1. As many as 59 iron objects are reported from Period II, and its has been noted that "iron starts occurring in the lowest levels of Period II". Only 4 of these 59 objects have been published by the excavator[21].

Fig. No.	Object	Context
64, 39	tanged spearhead	mid-level of Period I
64, 42	knife blade	late level of Period II
64, 43	ring	late level of Period II
64, 49	nail	late level of Period II

The excavator does not explain why he did not illustrate a single specimen from the lowest levels. However, elsewhere in the report we get the following [22]

"Its (i.e., of iron) extensive use is indicated by the find of 59 objects, beginning with a well-formed celt or chopper, from the earliest days. Among these the shapes of a spearhead, arrowheads, including a tanged type knife, blades, a ring or clamp for fastening a tool and socket of a possibly socketed axe, besides the chopper or celt mentioned above, point to the distinct divergent and specialized application iron of objects"

2. The excavator's opinion that there was a short break, 50 years,[23] in occupation between Period I and Period II at Nagda is belied by the soil analysis of the relevant "break" layer. We quote from the 'soil analysis' report by Dr. B.B. Lal [24]

"Sri N.R. Banerjee asked us to find out the nature of the formation of soil of Layer no. 9 which according to him is artificially laid, after the site remained abandoned for a while, but traces of the same cultural remains of earlier period, i.e., chalcolithic, were found in fair abudance even above this deposit. Similar infomation is sought for other layers".

On the basis of detailed studies of the soil submitted to him, Dr. B.B. Lal further wrote:

"In view of the above it is conclusive that the soil in the trench was deposited by slow moving water. The suggestion that layer no. 9 was deposited artificially cannot be proved in the light of the present observations as there is no contrasting difference among the composition of the soil samples from the trench.".

3. Period I at Nagda belongs to the Malwa chalcolithic and this phase came to an end around the middle of the second millennium BC or a little later. Banerjee [25] himself cites an uncalibrated radiocarbon date of 1370/100 BC for the overlap of the Malwa culture with the succeeding Jorwe culture at Daimabad in Maharashtra.

4. In view of the above there is no reason to doubt that the beginning of the iron-bearing Period II at Nagda falls in middle of the second millennium BC.

The stratigraphic situation from Nagda is supported by the sequence at Prakash on the Tapti and sites such as Eran in Malwa itself. The periodisation and chronology of Eran have been discussed by S.K. Pandey [26] who puts its Iron Age between 1300 and 700 BC.

IV. 4 The Megalithic Level of Peninsular India

Megaliths dominate the archaeology of almost the entire region from Berar in Maharasrtra in the north to the top of the Indian peninsula in the south. Chronologically this lies between *c.* 1000 BC and earlier, and at least the early centuries AD. There may be a pre-iron-using megalithic level in this region but this has not been firmly demonstrated yet. Certainly, there is no properly verified diagnostic archaeological evidence to divide this long phase over such a large region into sub-phases. In the present context we are concerned only with the iron-yielding megaliths and related settlement sites.

The earliest evidence so far has emerged from the Raichur Doab between the Krishna and the Tungabhadra rivers. Hallur[27] is located on the left bank of the Tungabhadra. The mound measures 500 m by 270 m, which makes it about 13.5 hectares in extent. The neolithic period or Period I at the site is divided into two phases. In the first phase, the main pottery types are 'pale grey and burnished ware'. The cultural items are fairly meagre: no lithic blade industry, rare polished stone tools, no house floor plan, one bone point, two pieces of antler and scarce 'minor' antiquities such as beads. In Phase 2, whose major ware is the 'brown-and-black ware', the repertoire is far more impressive: some Jorwe pottery, dolerite and trap polished stone axe industry, rich lithic black quartz industry, bone points, 62 beads (40 of shell, 15 of steatite, 1 of quartz, 1 of bone and 5 of terracotta). Copper objects are also found for the first time in this phase as are floors, double-urn burials and terracotta headrest and discs.

Period II at Hallur marks an overlap of the phase 2 of Period I ('neolithic-chalcolithic') and early Iron age. Except the lithic blade industry, the characteristic features of the phase 2 of Period I continue, with some additions. There are 3 main new types of pottery with two subvarieties: Black-and-Red ware which, with its highly burnished and polished surface, is a very distinctive megalithic ware of south India. The second variety is called 'All Black Ware', despite the fact that it is of the same fabric burnish and polish as the black-and-red ware. The third main variety is Red Ware (slipped and slightly polished; medium fabric; not well fired) occurring in a small quantity. A copper rod has been reported from Period II but about 17 iron objects have been described and illustrated for this period. These objects chiefly consist of arrowheads, spearheads, knife-blades and points. There are also seven beads and specimens of polished stone axe industry (axe, adze, chisel, wedge, rubber and grinder, hammer, etc.). The early historical material including pottery was found in the disturbed layers above Period II.

The uncalibrated radiocarbon dates from the 'overlap' phase or the phase of the early Iron Age are 1105/105 BC and 955/100 BC. The burials of the Iron Age—cairns and dolmenoid cist-circles—are found to the west of the site and to the north on the slopes of hilly tracts. The time-range indicated by these radiocarbon dates has been corroborated by thermoluminiscent dates from the megalithic burials at the site of Kumarnahalli in the same region. The excavation details are not available but thermoluminiscent dates have been published: 1470/290 BC; 1130/260 BC; 1160/500 BC; 960/470 BC; 1410/300 BC; 1230/280 BC; 1350/400 BC.

IV. 5 The Doab

Substantive evidence of the iron-bearing Painted Grey Ware culture of the Doab has been available since the publication of R.C. Gaur's excavation report of Atranjikhera on the bank of the Kali Nadi in the Aligarh district of western Uttar Pradesh.[28] Painted Grey Ware level at Atranjikhera has been divided into a number of phases and sub-phases "on the basis of floor-levels, statistical analysis of pottery and frequency of iron and other obejects", although, as the following statistical survey of pottery done by the excavator himself will show, the evidence of detailed phasing is not clear-cut.

Percentage of Pottery Occurrence in the Various Phases of the Painted Grey Ware Level at Atranjikhera

POTTERY	LOWER	MIDDLE, A	MIDDLE, B	UPPER
Black-and-Red	5.3	1.1	0.9	0.5
Black-slipped	15.6	1.1	2.0	2.8
Painted Grey	3.4	9.7	6.0	2.9
Grey	10.8	31.8	30.1	31.2
Red	64.9	56.3	61.0	62.6

On the basis of the frequency of Black-and-Red, Black-slipped and Grey wares, it is possible to make a differentiation between the 'lower' on the one hand, and the 'middle' and 'upper' phases on the other, but there does not seem to be much justification for distinguishing between the 'middle' and 'upper' phases. However, this chart convincingly demonstrates that the Painted Grey Ware, although the diagnostic trait of this layer, constituted only a small part of the total assemblage.

Seven structural sub-phases were found in the form of mud-floors. Both mud and mudbricks occur frequently whereas chunks of mud plaster with reed impressions are found in a much greater abundance. The general range of houses was no doubt in the form of wattle-and-daub constructions. The floors were usually made of fine yellowish compact earth, rammed in some cases with small pieces of mudbrick and burnt clay lumps. Postholes in the floors indicate the use of bamboo/wooden poles. Some floors have also been found associated with burnt patches, which may indicate cooking hearths. Also reported are several domestic hearths, fire-pits, furnaces (?) and potters' kilns.

In structural phase 2, associated with Gaur's lower phase of the culture, five clay floors revealed traces of burnt pebbles, circular fire-pits and U-shaped domestic hearths. Two better-preserved specimens showed the hearths to be semi-oval and 25-35 cm high. They had tapered sides with a curve at the top, "suggesting that usually big cooking vessels were used". A circular pit was found to contain ash, pieces of charcoal, grains and some small fragments of animal bones leading to its identification as a "sacrificial fire-pit".

In the third structural phase belonging to the 'middle' phase of the culture there is a well-preserved potter's kiln: roughly oval, 1 m deep and 2.35 m in diameter. "It yielded numerous pots with a rich variety of shape and design. The excavation revealed the alternate layers of pots and fuel (generally the cakes of animal dung) were arranged in the kiln and the top was fully covered with reeds and twigs, being finally closed with a mudplaster over them. Burnt plaster pieces with the impressions of above stuffs were found in large numbers which bear remarkable resemblance to similar plaster pieces in vogue in the village-pottery kiln even today."

Further, a circular pit in this structural phase "contained many small charred bones which had sharp cut marks. Among the animals killed at least one appeared to be a stag as a piece of its horn was found. Lumps of charred grains including pottery were also recovered. These finds strongly suggest that it was a sacrificial pit."

The upper phase of the culture phase 6 revealed a pear-shaped pit and some circular pits as well. These may be interpreted as blacksmith's furnaces because of their association with tapering clay lumps and finished iron tools.

Among the general antiquities there were beads of carnelian, marble, quartz and agate, miscellaneous whetstones, pestles, ball, etc., bone implements (arrowhead, stylus, pendant, etc.), pottery discs (plain or with impressed/incised crescent notches), distinctive ghat or pitcher shaped terracotta beads, and so on. There were also some objects of glass, shell and copper. The iron objects comprised a large number of types: arrowheads (21), spearheads (8), shafts (10), tongs (1), clamps (21), chisels (6), bars or rods (7), borers (6), needle (1), hooks (7), nails (20), axe (1), knives (3), bangles (2), slag (7) indeterminate fragments (14). There is no doubt that iron was a widely used material in the Painted Grey Ware level of the Indo-Gangetic divide and the upper Gangetic valley.

Towards its end, the Painted Grey Ware phase merged in the early historic assemblage of the *Doab* characterized by the NBP ware but its earlier point has been subject to some controversy. On the basis of an uncalibrated radiocarbon date from Atranjikhera the beginning of this period at the site has been put around 1100 BC. On the basis of similarly uncalibrated dates from this period at other sites some scholars prefer to bring down the general beginning of the Painted Grey Ware to c. 800 BC. For a very clear reason, we support the earlier date of its beginning. It must be remembered that around the middle of the second millennium Bc, and later the Doab must have witnessed the simultaneous occurrence of a number of ceramic traditions: the late Harappan and the related Ochre Coloured Pottery (OCP) complex, Black-and-Red Ware phase and finally, Painted Grey Ware phase. Stratigraphically, their occurrence is successive, but we forget their chronological range may be significantly overlapping. For instance, the succession of the late Harappan phase by an overlapping phase of grey ware in Haryana and eastern Punjab cannot be denied. What is more interesting is that there is a single specimen of an etched carnelian bead in the Black and Red Ware context of Atrajikhera, indicating a kind of continuation of the late Harappan tradition. Moreover, the thermoluiminiscent dates of the OCP complex at Atranjikhera and other *Doab* sites put them in the first quarter of the second millennium BC. There is, in fact, really no reason why the Painted Grey Ware tradition of the *Doab* should not begin by the last quarter of the second millennium BC.

IV. 6 Eastern India

The chalcolithic Black-and-Red Ware level in the middle and lower Gangetic valley developed in the background of an extensive neolithic level which can be pushed back into the third millenium BC. The chalcolithic level itself possibly dates, at its earliest, from the second quarter of the second millennium BC. Iron appears as a part of this black-and-red ware column which continues uninterrupted into the early historic phase of the region which began around 600 BC or earlier. The iron-bearing levels in Bihar are not yet independently dated, but at least three sites in West Bengal - Bahiri [29] Pandu Raja Dhibi and Mangalkot[30] yield dates around 1000 BC for their first iron-bearing levels.

We concentrate on the data from Mangalkot. Its periodization is as follows: In Period I, "the most important discovery of this phase is the evidence regarding the use of iron, right from the bottom layer of this cultural period" [31] Period II is transitional, between the chalcolithic and early historical - "The important finds of this phase consist of iron objects in profuse number like arrowhead, chisel, sickle, knife-points indicating increasing use of iron technology. This is substantiated by the discovery of huge oven like space, covered with thick layer of ash containing a large quantity of iron slags and half-finished iron tools, indicating smelting of iron in the site". The inventory also includes mud floors with post holes, plastered with cow dung - at times rammed with potsherd, kankars and soil, wattle-and-daub construction, human figure in a highly generalized form in terracotta, bead, disc, net-sinkers, bangle, two microlithic blade-bone tools, arrowheads, blades, scrapers, dagger, points, awls, axe type small objects, lunate made of antler, and tortoise shell. There is a spiral bangle with 10% tin, and among the iron objects there is a point, spearhead, knife, lump and slag. In the transitional phase occur an iron spearhead, sickle point, knife, broken portion of a crucible, slag and lumps. The faunal remains include fish and turtle, two species of deer, pigeon, fowl, cattle, buffalo, and pig with cut marks as also *turbinella pyrum* shell.

The so-called neolithic level of Barudih in Singhbhum district (Bihar) has also yielded an iron sickle. This occurs in a level marked by a profusion of neolithic celts, and coarse black-and-red pottery. The earliest available date is 1055/210 BC (calibrated 1410-830 BC).

V. Consequences

Iron technology is a loaded term in discussions of early socio-economic transformations in India - to the extent that this technological invention is considered to be the harbinger of various 'revolutionary' modifications in agriculture, artisanal production, settlement patterns and management of ancient economies, etc. In the last few decades, however, the Indian data base for the Iron Age has greatly expanded, as has the disenchantment with existing and rather rigid, explanatory models that have generally taken it for granted that this was a highly 'consequential' transition point in Indian history. We believe that the most useful method for undertaking an assessment of the issue is by looking at iron in its total cultural context in different subregions rather than as an entity possessing its own uniform dynamic. The previous section has already indicated the general changes and continuities in the cultural assemblage of pre-and Iron Age levels. Here, we examine this problem of continuity versus change in the transition from copper to bronze with reference to primarily four variables, successively enumerated, as far as possible, for each region - (i) site distribution, (ii) plant and animal remains, (iii) specific raw material usage, and (iv) interaction spheres. These variables are outlines on the basis of published information (synthesizes in Chakrabarti[32] and Lahiri[33] The focus of this section is on those neolithic - chalcolithic contexts which in the published reports of their respective areas are shown to be stratigraphically prior in relation to the succeeding Iron age levels. The Iron Age levels that we discuss are those which are known to antedate the historical phase and, we propose to show that by foregrounding the above mentioned four variables, a more realistic evaluation of the consequences of a transition from the neolithic-chalcolithic to the iron using cultures is possible.

V.1 Archaeological Data

North-West

KASHMIR

Neolithic-Chalcolithic: (i) More than 50 well distributed sites, including many in the valley portion, with a concentration in the Baramulla area. (ii) At Gufkral, [34a] wheat, barley, common pea, lentil. Domesticated and wild sheep and goat, wild and domesticated cattles, ibex, red deer, fowl. (iii) Steatite, carnelian, agate, copper/bronze, trap and sandstone artefacts. (iv) Indus plains links evident from presence of a globular pot with horned deity (resembling similar types at Kot Diji and Gumla) at Burzahom and a single spiral headed copper pin from Gufkral. Common ceramic elements between Kashmir neolithic-chalcolithic and that of Swat. *Iron Age*: (i) Such horizons seem to be substantially less and details of them shadow; apart from Gufkral, noteworthy iron-bearing megalithic sites are Baramulla and Dwi-Ekam-pura. (ii) Domesticated rice and possibly cultivated millet at Gufkral, (iii) Copper, iron, bone. (iv) No specific evidence of interregional interaction.

North west frontier highlands and lowlands

Neolithic-Chalcolithic: (i) Dir, Swat, Chitral, Ghorband, Buner and the Peshawar lowlands. (ii) Three types of barley, also rice, wheat, lentil, peas, and hackberry. 18 forms of fauna at Loebanr (iii) and Aligrama (iv) including porcupine, hare, dog, wild cat, tiger, ass, half ass, horse, camel, pig, deer species, probably water buffalo, zebu, goral (*Nemorhedus goral,* markhor (*Capra falconeri)*, domestic goat and sheep. Predominance of domestic animals (iii) Copper/bronze, gold, silver, lapis lazuli, jade, marine shell, ivory, carnelian, agate, alabaster, onyx, chalcedony, schist, granite, limestone, quartzite, serpentine. (iv) Ceramic affinities with Kashmir on the one hand and post-Harappan Cemetery H pottery,. Artefactual similarities (stone shaft holed axes, harvesters, bone pin and painted representation on pottery from Bir-kot-ghundai) with China and northern Afghanistan (copper/bronze objects and ceramic similarities in pottery with Dashli I) as well. *Iron Age*; (i) Gandhara Grave Culture distributed in the area north-northeast of Peshawar and extending upto Chitral. (ii) Agricultural base, including cultivation of rice. (iii) Copper/bronze, iron, silver, gold, glass, schist, slate, magnesite, quartz, granite, shell, ivory, carnelian, agate, lapis lazuli. (iv) Iron cheek-bar at Timargarha typologically similar to those groups which played role in the steppe-belt between the 10th and 6th centuries BC [34b].

BALUCHISTAN

Neolithic-Chalcolithic: (i) Pirak, 20 kms east of Nausharo, only well known site with chalcolithic and early iron bearing levels[35].(ii) Multicropping system-Winter cereals (wheat and barley), summer crops (rice, millet and sorghum). Rice indicates' introduction of a permanent irrigation system. Horse, donkey and camel. (iii) Sickle flint elements, copper/bronze, bone, ivory, antler, sea shells. (iv) Similarities in metal artefacts with Central Asia (convex disks with a loop, drillings rasps, strainers). *Iron Age*; (i) Occupation still limited to Pirak. (ii) No changes in subsistence mentioned by the excavators. (iii) Iron, copper/bronze. Also, sickle flint elements in the first phase of iron usage.

West India

Neolithic-chalcolithic: (i) Ahar type site of the Banas culture which is distributed over the Malpura-Karauli plain (over 50 sites). In northeast Rajasthan, the metallurgical complex of Ganeshwar-Jodhpura with over 70 sites; main concentration in the Sikar district with some sites in Jhunjhunu and Jaipur. (ii) At Ahar, rice staple cereal and animal bones include fish, *Bos Indicus*, domestic goat, domestic sheep, *barasingha, Sus cristatus* (var domesticus), wild boar, and domestic dog. At Ganeshwar, animal bones include those of cattle, fish, fowl, sheep and goat. (iii) In Period Ia faience, terracotta and schist beads known at Ahar, in addition to artefacts made from copper and local stones. Ganeshwar-Jodhpura complex's main artefacts of copper with quartz, chalcedony, jasper, and garnet microliths. (iv) The Ganeshwar metallurgical complex's links with the Harappan Civilization obvious from presence of Harappan pottery in Sikar and Jhunjhunu; copper celts at Sabania with Indus script; general affinities in the shapes of some copper based artefacts. *Iron Age:* The two successive phases of the Black and red ware culture (Ib and IC) of Ahar are iron bearing as is the black-and red ware deposit at Noh. The situation at the latter site is intriguing in the sense that in areas towards the east, i.e. in the Indo-Gangetic divide and the Upper Gangetic plains, black-and red ware deposits are generally iron free. In Rajasthan, not enough has been published on this culture to allow us to ascertain cultural changes or continuities. (i) No specific evidence on the issue of settlement distribution. (ii) Rice continues to be important at Ahar. Vishnu Mittre's analysis suggested the presence of millet in the iron bearing levels (Period Ib and Ic), although Sankalia added a cautionary note in this regard. While the earlier animal remains continue, two new species introduced in Period Ib-c are Indian domestic buffalo and fowl. Among the raw materials, in addition to copper and iron in Periods Ib and Ic agate, bone, calcite, carnelian, crystal, faience, glass, jasper, lapis, schist, shell, steatite and terracotta beads. (iv) Very clear affinities of Ahar Ib-c with the Harappan distribution area (noted earlier).

Central India

Neolithic-chalcolithic: (i) Over a 100 such sites even in 1967 [36] (ii) Dietary range of such sites evident from Period I at Nagda: humped cattle, goats, sheep, and pigs some with cut marks and unspecified 'hard grains'. (ii) steatite, shell, coral, ivory, jade, lapis, gold, copper/bronze, ordinary and semi-precious stones. (iv) presence of late Harappans in Malwa. *Iron Age:* (i) Period II at Nagda and Period IIA at Eran seem to be really culturally continuous with the chalcolithic levels, with the additional presence of iron. (ii) 'Hard grains' consumed. Animal species include three turtle varieties, domestic cat, Indian domestic cattle and sheep. (iii) Ivory, copper, iron, carnelian, agate, jade, coral and bone. (iv) Nothing specific known.

Peninsular India

Neolithic-chalcolithic: Hallur (Karanataka) may be taken as the index site. (i) Hallur's Period I cultural elements well distributed in Karnataka. (ii) Two varieties of millet (*Eleusine coracana* and *Paspalum scrobiculatum)*, rice, fruits of teak tree, cattle, deer and mollusc. (iii) Dolerite, schist, trap, quartzite, copper shell, quartz, steatite and bone at Hallur. (iv) At Hallur, limited sherds of Jorwe ware and huge jars in a coarse grey ware of Nevasa type. *Iron Age:* Considerable cultural continuity, including pottery, plant and faunal remains. Raw materials used include bone, carnelian, terracotta, gold, green stone, antler, copper and iron.

We are aware that there are a large number of neolithic-chalcolithic horizons in this entire area around Tekkalakota alone 19 of them were reported. The artefactual repertoires of many such sites in Karnataka are also very impressive, associated with rich ground stone axe industries is a microlithic blade element and beads of steatite, coral, miscellaneous semi-precious stones, an elaborate gold ear ornament (Tekkalakota) and terracotta objects. Similarly in Andhra, such horizons have yielded copper, shell, steatite, semi-precious stones, including agate and opal, etc. This complex is also linked in various ways with Maharashtra and similar complexes in Tamil Nadu and Karnataka.

As for the iron-bearing megalithic levels of this zone, those of the Vidarbha region are suggestive of rich agricultural settlements and their beginning can be dated to around the 8th century BC. However, there is no antecedent neolithic-chalcolithic level at these sites which would permit us to make a realistic comparison. If we look at Maharashtra in general, apart from the introduction of iron, in terms of the range of raw materials, distribution of settlements and interregional interactions, the preceding neolithic-chacolithic horizons are equally impressive. The situation is more complex with reference to the megaliths in regions to the south of Maharashtra. There are thousands of megalithic sites ranging from 1000 BC to the early centuries AD. An excellent study of such sites has been published by U.S. Moorti [37] who has postulated a ranked society during this 'period'. But then, 'which period' is being referred to? Some of Moorti's 1900 odd megalithic sites are very early while others date to the 2nd century AD. The problem lies here.

Doab

Neolithic-chalcolithic: The pre-iron age horizons in this context are the Ochre Coloured Pottery (OCP) and Black-and-Red ware (BRW) levels. (i) OCP sites in Saharanpur, Meerut, Bulandshahr, Muzaffarnagar, Moradabad, Etah, Aligarh and Etawah. BRW horizons in Etawah, Kanpur, Aligarh, Budaun and Bulanshahr districts. (ii)Rice, barley, gram, *Kesari* and cattle bones with cut marks in OCP phase at Atranjikhera. Rice and barley continue at the same site into the BRW level. (iii) Raw materials from several sites (Gandhrona, Ambkheri, Bargaon, Saipai, Lal Qila, Jakhera and Atranjikhera) include shell, chert, sandstone, quartzite, chalcedony, agate, carnelian, copper/bronze and several types of timber such as teak and *chir* pine which have central India and the Uttar Pradesh hills as their respective distribution area. (iv) Pottery at several sites with Harappan parallels. The presence of an etched carnelian bead at Atranjikhera also underlines this connection. *Iron Age*: (i) PGW sites in Saharanpur, Bijnor, Mathura, Agra, Farukhabad, Muzaffarnagar, Mainpuri, Meerut, Etawah, Budaun, Unnao, Hardoi, Etah, Moradabad, Bulandshahr, Lucknow and Aligarh. (ii) Wheat introduced into the existing crop pattern. Also fowl, river turtle, bull, pig, goat, deer, horse and possibly fish. (iii) Copper, iron, glass, bone, agate, jasper, carnelian, and chalcedony. Abundant iron artefacts at sites like Atranjikhera (iv) Close links with the middle Gangetic plains on the one hand and the northwest on the other.

Eastern India

Neolithic-chalcolithic: Hallmark of chalcolithic assemblage is a plain and painted black-and-red ware which is found in association with a number of other ceramic types such as black and black-slipped wares, red and red-slipped wares, buff ware etc. (i) Wide, distribution. In Bengal alone, 80 reported sites. (ii) Rice in Bengal and Bihar. Most impressive evidence from Senuar: rice, barley, dwarf wheat, bread wheat, sorghum millet, chick pea, green gram or *moong*, field pea, lentil, horse gram, grass peas, sesamum and linseed. (iii) Copper, steatite, ivory, sandstone, chert, quartzite, basalt, chert, granite, chalcedony, agate, jasper, and soapstone. *Iron Age*: Continuity of culture and agricultural history with iron being introduced into the existing black-and-red ware phase.

V.2 Conclusions

The issue that has to be evaluated, on the basis of the above mentioned evidence, is whether the use of iron in protohistoric India (by 1000 BC in many areas) led to a qualitatively different economy and society. The evidence is admittedly uneven in scope and detail, but, nevertheless allows for a few generalizations.

(a) It is mainly in the *Doab* and Kashmir, that the first iron-using cultures are easily distinguishable because of their diagnostic pottery. In the eastern and central protions of India, there is nothing specific to argue that there was a cultrual break/development with the advent of iron. As far as one can see, it is the same assemblage of plain and painted black-and-red and associated wares, microliths, some copper and iron. In the northwest also, there is no cultural break. In south India, at Hallur, the situation is similar although on the whole in that region the evidence is more complex. This is because of a number of neolith/

megalith overlap levels where the date of the beginning of iron is sometime before 1000 BC but how does one know, without excavation, that a particular megalithic iron-mixed assemblage is early or not. The megaliths, nevertheless, while containing a number of elements which have neolithic-chalcolithic antecedents, also seem to mark a distinct phase mainly by virtue of the creation of large stone monuments that are its most distinguishing feature.

(b) With regard to Kashmir, the cultural break notwithstanding, the iron bearing megaliths are a very shadowy entity, especially in relation to the antecedent flourishing neolithic-chalcolithic horizons. As far as the *doab* is concerned, with the appearance of Painted Grey Ware, there is a definite burgeoning of settlements. But, what needs to be assessed is whether there is a change in the distribution pattern of such settlements. The Kanpur district, which has been closely researched may be taken as the index region. The number of such sites located by Makkhan Lal[38] in Kanpur district is 40, all located on the river banks with the exception of five located near low-lying areas—this is in broad continuity of the earlier distribution of BRW settlements. A shift away from river banks takes place only in the historical NBP ware phase.

(c) As for the subsistence base, the crop pattern of the entire Indian subcontinent, barring some exceptions, seems to have been laid down in the earlier chalcolithic stage. In fact, it would be accurate to state that possibly not a single crop was added to the list after iron was introduced. It is true that rice is introduced into the iron bearing megalithic horizon of Kashmir while at Atranjikhera, wheat is added to the diet in the PGW phase. At the same time, these are only new crop elements in terms of the local site situation. In the larger regional situations, these crops were present prior to the iron bearing levels. In the case of the Indo-Gangetic divide and the Upper Gangetic plains where Atranjikhera stood, even in the late Harappan context wheat was a part of the agricultural regime of farmers at Mohrana in Punjab and Hulas in Saharanpur. The crop list of late Harappan Hulas underlines the secure subsistence base of neolithic-chalcolithic farmers quite clearly: rice, barley, dwarf wheat, bread wheat, club wheat, oats, sorghum/jowar, ragi/finger millet, lentil, some varieties of fruits and wild grasses.

(d) There is also no sudden efflorescence of trade and interregional interaction with the advent of iron. In some cases such as Ahar and the Painted Grey Ware phase of the *doab* the scale increases. But even there, as in other parts of India, the peasant groups of neolithic-chalcolithic India, like the later Iron Age farmers, had interchanged artefacts and raw materials with each other and utilized resources ranging from wood to metal with source areas outside their immediate hinterlands.

(e) What may be briefly assessed as well is the role of copper-bronze in iron-bearing contexts since the "Iron Age" has sometimes been understood as marking the advent of a technology which (a) significantly reduced copper usage and (b) objects of which *replaced all* functional artefactual categories of earlier copper based metals. We refer here to the Hastinapur and Atranjikhera metallic repertoires. Hastinapur in its iron-bearing layer has yielded many more copper based artefacts as compared to iron. While the Painted Grey Ware level has yielded iron ore and slags, but no objects, there are a number of copper and bronze objects in that period, including an arrowhead, borer, nail parer, etc. A clearer picture is available from Atranjikhera in the Upper Gangetic valley where, with reference to the first iron-bearing level (Period III;PGW) the excavator has argued that "the introduction of iron, which was the most suitable metal for arms and implements drastically reduced the use of copper" [39] In view of the metallic objects that are cited in the report, this conclusion may be considered premature. The Black-and-red ware horizon at Artanjikhera, which contains no iron has yielded only a few non-utilitarian copper objects: broken ring, 3 beads. However, in the iron age PGW level, there are 22 copper objects which increase in number from the lower (3 objects) through the middle (6 objects) to the upper phases (13 objects). These include celt, fish-hook, nail-parer, antimony rod-cum-nail parer, pin, dish, bangle, ring and antimony rod. These data suggest that while the role that copper and its alloys had in chalcolithic contexts must have been supplemented and modified by the presence of a new metal in the Iron Age, there does not seem to be an immediate and widespread replacement of copper/bronze with iron.

An efficient technology does not automatically make for social complexity. In assessing the consequences of the Iron Age, we have tried to show that the technological element should not be interpreted as an abstract component. When viewed in its total cultural context, iron does not seem to have given a 'revolutionary' or qualitatively different dimension to the pattern of protohistoric growth in the Indian subcontinent. The notion of the Iron Age representing a major social and economic transformation, as much as it may appeal to our love of a neatly ordered succession of events working in tandem with technological change, in the light of the data we have cited, does not stand to historical scrutiny.

REFERENCES

1. Chakrabarti, D.K. 1992. *The Early use of iron in India.* Delhi.

2a. Cooke, S.R.B. and Aschenbrenner,S. 1975. The occurrence of metallic iron in ancient copper. *Journal of Field Archaeology* 2(3):251-66.

2b. Charles,J.A. 1979. From Copper to Iron-the origin of metallic materials. Posnansky, M. 1982. African Archaeology comes of Age. *World Archaeology*-13: 345-58. Pigott, V. The Iron Age in western Iran, *The coming of the Age of Iron.* New Haven *Journal of Metals 30:8-13.*

3. Sahi,M.D.N. 1979. Iron at Ahar, *Essays in Indian Protohistory* (ed. D.P. Agrawal and D.K. Chakrabarti). Delhi:365-6.

———— 1980. Origin of Iron Metallurgy in India. *Proceedings of the Indian History Congress.* Delhi.

Sankalia, H.D. Deo, S.B. and Ansari Z. (1969). *Excavations at Ahar.* Poona.

4. Fairservis,W. (1973). Preliminary Report on Excavations at Allahadino (First Season-1973). *Pakistan Archaeology*:95-102.

5. Shaffer,J.G. (1978). Bronze Age Iron from Afganistan: its Implications for South Asian Protohistory. Mimeographed paper.

6. Ghosh,A.ed. 1989. *An Encyclopaedia of Indian Archaeology.* Volume 1. p.319 New Delhi.

7. Yule, P. (1989). *The Copper Hoards of the Indian Subcontinent, Preliminaries for an interpretation.* Mainz. p.262.

8. Chakrabarti,D.K. and Lahiri,N. (n.d.) The Early use of Copper and its alloys in India.

9. Yule,P. (1985). *Metalwork of the Bronze Age in India.* Munich.p.54.

10. Yule, P. 1989. Op.cit. p.36

11. Lahiri, N. (n.d.) The alloying traditions of protohistoric and historic India: Some general trends and their ethnographic dimensions.

Lal,M. (1984). *Settlement History and Rise of Civilisation in Ganga-Yamuna Doab.* Delhi.

12. Pigot,V. (1980). The Iron Ag in Western Iran. *The Coming of the Age of Iron.* New Haven.

13. De Terra,H.H. and Paterson.T.T. 1939. *Studies on the Ice Age in India and Associated Human cultures.* Washington.

14. Jarrige,J.F. and Enault,J.P. 1973 *Radiocarbon and Indian Archaeology* (ed.D.P. Agrawal and A. Ghosh):391-400.

15. Stacul,G.1969. Excavation near Ghaligai (1968) and chronological sequence of Protohistorical cultures in the Swat Valley. *East and West* 19;44-91.

16. Hooja,R. 1988. *The Ahar Culture.* Oxford.

17. IAR 1971-72; 42.

18. IAR 1970-71: 31-32.

19. Rao,S.R. 1985. Lothal: *A Harappan Port Town.* New Delhi.

20. Banerjee, N.R. 1986. Nagda Excavations. Delhi.

21. Op. Cit., fig. 64, nos. 39, 42, 43, 49.

22. *op. cit.* 27-280.

23. op. cit.

24. op. cit. 276.

25. op. cit. preface.

Chakrabarti,D.K. 1985. The issues of the Indian Iron Age, in *Recent Advances in Indian Archaeology* (ed. S.B. Deo and K.V. Paddayya). Pune: 74-77.

26. Pandey,S.K. 1982. Chalcolithic Eran and its Chronology. IANP:249-56.

27. Nagaraja Rao,M.S. 1971. *Protohistoric cultures of the Tungabhadra valley....* Dharwar.

28. Gaur,R.C. 1983. *Excavations at Atranjikhera.* Delhi.

29. Chakrabarti, D.K. and Hasan,S.J. 1982. The Sequence at Bahiri...*Man and Environment* 6:111-49.

30 Ray, A. and Mukherjee, S.K. 1992. Excavation at Mangalkot. *Pratna Samiksha* 1:107-34.

31. Op. cit.

32. Chakrabarti, D.K. 1994. The Archaeology of Ancient Ind*ian Cities.* Delhi.

33. Lahiri,N. 1992. *The Archaeology of Indian Trade Routes upto 200 BC.* Delhi.

34a. Sharma,A.K. (1991a). Excavations in Kashmir. Journal of Marine Archaeo*logy* 2:79-82.

34b. Jettmar,K. 1967. An Iron cheek-piece and snaffle found at Timargarha. *Ancient Pakistan* 3:203-9.

————(1991b). Antiquity of Iron from Gufkral. *Recent Advances in Marine Archaeology*:181-82.

35. Jarriage, J.F. 1985. Continuity and change in the North Kachi Plain... *South Asian Archaeology* 1983: 35-68.

36. Wakankar,V.S. (1982). Chalcolithic Malwa. Indian Archaeology: New Perspectives (R.K. Sharma). Delhi:224-37.

37. Moorti,U.S. (1991). Evidence of social differentiation and sociopolitical organization during the megalithic period in south India. *Puratattva* 20: 1-64.

37. ——————(1994). *Megalithic Culture of South India —Socio-economic perspectives*. Varanasi.

38. Mackay,E.J.H. (1938). Further excavations *at Mohenjodaro*. 2 volumes. Delhi.

39. Op.cit.p.230

40. Krishnan,M.S. (1954). *Iron Ore, Iron and Steel*. Bulletin of the Geological Survey of India. Delhi.

CHART 1

DISTRIBUTION OF IRON-ORES AND THE PRE-INDUSTRIAL SMELTING TRADITION IN THE INDIAN SUBCONTINENT

(after Krishnan 1952, Chakrabarti 1992, Lahiri 1992)

Region & Locality	Nature of Ore	Details of Preindustrial tradition
Jammu & Kashmir : Matah, Gangani, Ladda, Khandli	magnetite, haematite, limonite	limonite smelting, especially in the Sof area
Baluchistan : Sanni in Kacchi, Kumbi to the West of Kotra	ferrous sulphate (zogh)	Zagh mining; extracted mineral used for black dye & graining swords
North West Frontier Bajaur, Hazara, Bannu Waziri hills, Chitral	magnetic iron sand, haematite, limonite, magnetie	haematite smelting in Bannu, magnetic iron sand from Bajaur smelted at Peshwar
Sind: Kohistan-Ranikot	magnetite, haematite	
Potwar & West Punjab: Salt range, Kot Kira-ana hills, Mianwali, Sargodha and Attock	haematite, laterite	low grade laterite smelting in Salt range
Himachal: Kangra, Simla, Mandi, Sirmur, Kulu	magnetic ore, micacaous ore, haematite,	smelting in Kangra, Kulu & Simla hill states; superior quality from Kangra, known to break at only 61300 lbs per sq. inch
Uttar Pradesh Nainital, Almora, Garhwal, Mirzapur	haematite, iron stone, magnetite, magnetic sand	haematite smelting in Kumaun, Garhwal, Almora, Nainital; Agaria smelters in Mirzapur
Rajasthan: Alwar, Bundi, Jaipur,Udaipur, Ajmer, Bharatpur, Jodhpur, Kota, Bhilwara	haematite, magnetite, limonite, ilmenite, ferruginous breccia	numerous old working & furnaces in Alwar, Bundi, Jodhpur, Udaipur using deposits ranging from haematite to breccia

East Punjab& Haryana: Patiala Narnaul, Dhanauta-Dhancholi, Firozpur	haematite, magnetite	smelting in Patiala & Firozpur
Bihar: Hazaribagh, Singhbhum, Ranchi, Palamau, Mungher, Santal, Paraganas, Bhagalpur, Ranchi	titaniferous magnetite, ilmenite, haematite, laterite, schists, iron stone	schist &laterite smelting in Singhbhum; iron stone smelting in Hazaribagh; native smething Imelting in most ore bearing zones; remnants of Asura iron smelters still present in Ranchi
Orissa: Mayurbhanj, Keonjhar, Bonai, Talcher, Sambhalpur	laterite, magnetite, haematite	smelting in Sambalpur & Talcher
West Bengal: Purulia, Midnapur, Bankura, Birbhum, Darjeeling	haematite, magnetite, titaniferous ores, siderite, limonite, laterite te, haematitic quartzite	smelting in Birbhum & adjacent areas
North-East: Assam (Lakhimpur & Sibsagar) Meghalaya (Khasi-Jantia)	clay iron stone, limonite, weathered granites	Assam iron traditionally used there cannon & small arms manufacture; Khashi iron considered of very superior quality; extensive preindustrial traditions in north-east
Central India: Ujjain, Shajapur, Shivpuri, Mandasore, Gwalior, Indore, Dhr, Narsinghpur,-Rewa, Hoshangabad, Nimar, Bastar, Chanda, Durg, Jabalpur, Bilaspur, Banda, Mandla, Bundelkhand	laterite, iron bearing Kaimur sandstone haematite shale, iron stone shale, brecciated ore, haematite, ferruginous schist, 'float' ore, micaceous ore, pisoltic limonite	extensive evidence of smelting at Bastar, Bilaspur, Raipur (haematite & laterite), Chanda (haematite), Balaghat (haematite), Bhandara (laerite), Mandla (laterite), Seoni, Chhindwara (laterite), Hoshangabad (haematite), Narsinghpur (maganiferous haematite & limonite), Jabalpur (maganiferous haematite), Bundelkhand (haematite)
Maharashtra & Goa: Ratnagiri, Kolhapur, Mahabaleshwar, Goa Amraoti, Nagpur, Chandrapur, Bhandara,	laterite, maganiferous ore, haematite quartzite, ferruginous earth, ferruginous sand, haematite, limonite	smelting in Ratnagiri, Satara
Gujarat: Surat, Panchmahal, Rewakantha, Ahmedabad, Kutch-Kathiawar, Broach	iron stone, laterite, magnetic sand, limonite,	smelting in Rewakantha, Saurashta; slag heaps at Kaira & Ahmedabad

Karnataka: Kanara, Tumkur, Mysore, Chitaldurg, Kolar, Shimoga, Bellary, Bijapur, Raichur, Chik--magalur	laterite, haematite quartzites, titaniferous ore, magnetic sand, ferruginous schist	magnetite & laterite smelting at Malabar, haematite smelting at Bellary, 'black sand' smelting at Mysore
Andhra; Cuddaph, Kurnool, Guntur, West Godavari, Krishna, Vishakapatnam, Hyderabad. Adilabad, Anantapur, Prakasam	magnetite quartzite, haematite, limonite	haematite mining in Cuddapah & Kurnool, smelt ing in Guntur, Godavari, Vishakapatnam
Kerala: Calicut, Kottayam, Malappuram, Palghat, Quilon, Trichur, Cannanore, Coorg	ferruginous quartzite, laterite, magnetite, iron stone	preindustrial smelting in Travancore & Malabar
Tamil Nadu: Salem Dharmapuri, South Arcot, Tiruchirapalli, North Arcot, Coimbatore, Madurai	magnetite, haematite, laterite, specular ore	smelting in Salem, South & North Arcot, Chingleput & Coimbatore; slag heaps in Madurai andTiruchirappalli

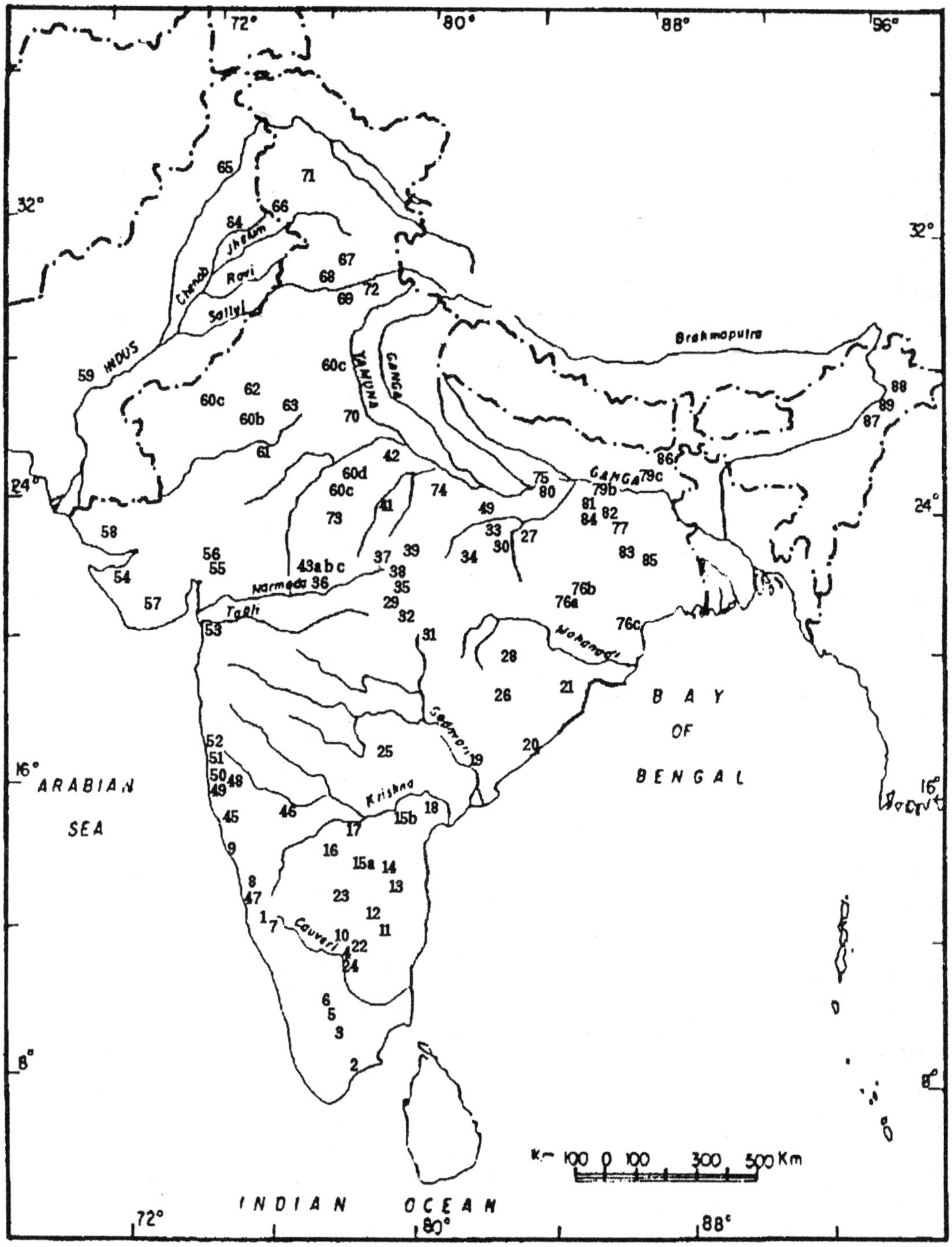

Fig 1: Distribution of Pre-industrial Iron-smelting

Fig 1: Distribution of Pre-industrial Iron-smelting

1. Travancore
2. Tirunevelli
3. Madurai
4. Pudukottai
5. Thiruchirapalli
6. Coimbatore
7. Nilgiri Hills
8. Malabar
9. South Kanara
10. Salem
11. South Arcot
12. North Arcot
13. Chingleput
14. Nellore

15a. Cuddapah

15b. Kurnool

16. Anantapur
17. Bellary
18. Krishna
19. Godavari
20. Vishakhapatnam
21. Ganjam
22. Ashtagram Division, Mysore
23. Bangalore Division
24. Nagar, Mysore
25. Hyderabad
26. Bastar
27. Bilaspur
28. Raipur
29. Chanda
30. Balaghat
31. Bhandara
32. Nagpur
33. Mandla
34. Seoni
35. Chhindwara
36. Nimar
37. Hoshangabad
38. Narshangabad
39. Jabalpur
40. Rewa
41. Bundelkhand
42. Gwalior

43a. Indore

43b. Dhar

43c. Chandgarh, Indore

44. Ali Rajpur, Indore
45. Dharwar
46. Dharwar
47. Kaladgi
48. Belgaum
49. Goa
50. Sawantipur and Kolhapur
51. Ratnagiri
52. Satara
53. Surat
54. Rawakantha
55. Panchmahals
56. Kaira and Ahmedabad
57. Kathiawar
58. Kutch
59. Sind

60a. Narwar

60b. Ajmer

60c. Bundi

60d. Kota

60e. Bharatpur

61. Mewar
62. Jaipur
63. Alwar

64. Bannu
65. Peshawar
66. Kot Kirana Hills
67. Kangra
68. Mandi
69. Simla Hills
70. Gurgaon
71. Kashmir
72. Kumaun
73. Lalitpur
74. Banda
75. Mirzapur
76a. Cuttack
76b. Talcher
76c. Dhenkanal
77. Burdwan
78. Birbhum
79a. Bhagalpur
79b. Monghyr
80. Gaya
81. Hazaribagh
82. Purulia/Manbhum
83. Singhbhum
84. Lohardaga
85. Chhotanagpur Tributary States
86. Darjeeling
87. Khasi-Jaintia Hills
88. Naga Hills
89. Manipur

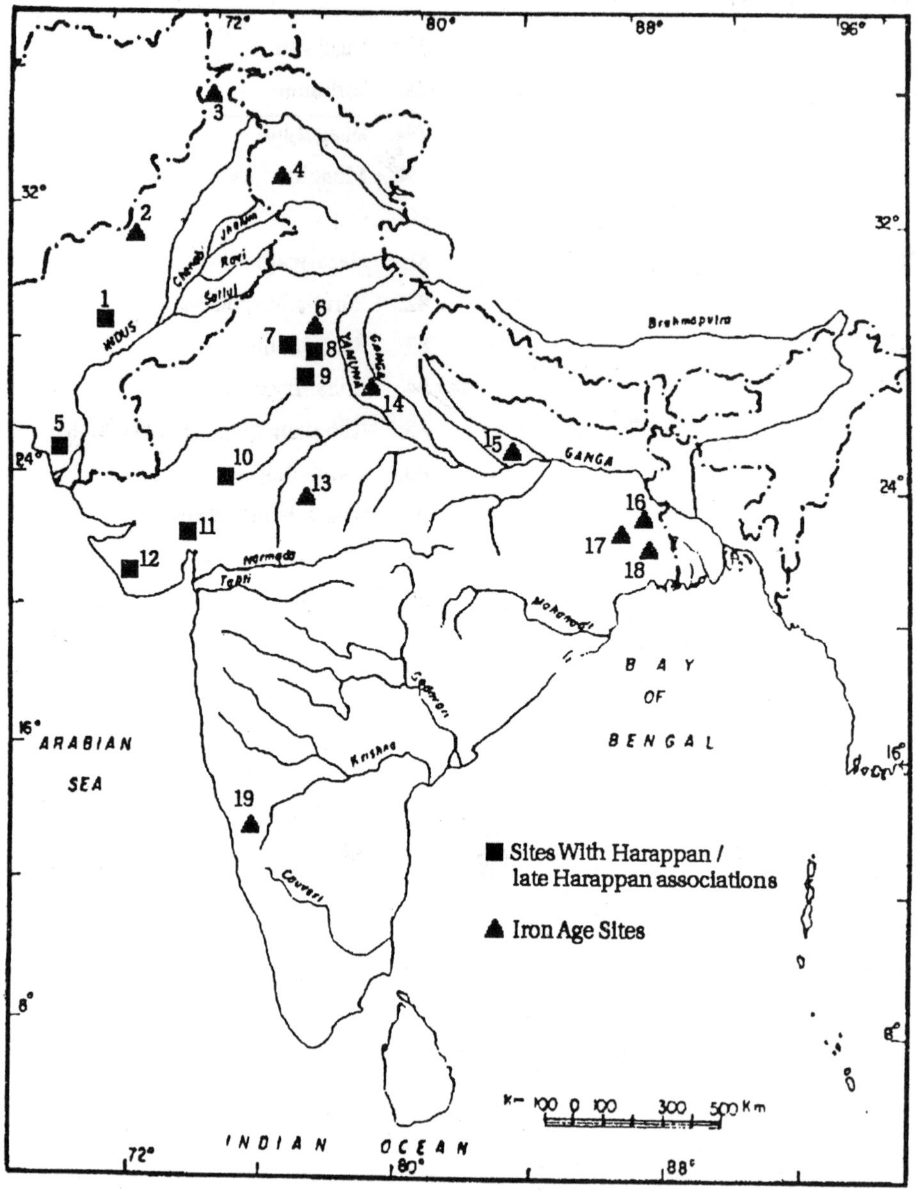

Fig 2: Major Sites Mentioned in the Paper

1. Mohenjodaro
2. Pirak
3. Gandhara Grave Culture
4. Gufkral
5. Allahadino
6. Noh
7. Hansi
8. Bhiwani
9. Rewari
10. Ahar
11. Lothal
12. Somnath
13. Nagda
14. Atranjikhera
15. Chirand
16. Bahiri
17. Mangalkot
18. Pandu Raja Dhibi
19. Hallur

NOTES AND NEWS

A Report on the Discovery of a Palaeolithic Site Near Katra, Udhampur District, Jammu

Jammu Siwaliks is bound in the Northwest by an antecedent river Chenab. Besides, another major river Tawi divides the city of Jammu. Compared to river Chenab, river Tawi has a shorter course and origin in the Inner Himalayas. Both the rivers, particularly river Tawi, flow through the hilly Siwalik tract. Most of this tract is sparsely vegetated, thereby giving the name *kandi*. As one proceeds northward from the plains, highly erosive steep south facing scarps are noticed. Vegetational cover improves towards the north and pine (*Pinus losifolia*) growth is noticed deep inside the Siwalik terrain.

Five terraces were recognised on rivers Chenab and Tawi, and equated to the glacial and interglacial phases of Pleistocene glacial sequence of Alps. The evidences of Early Man in the form of lithic artefacts were first noticed on these terrace surfaces[1]. Subsequently, investigations in the NW Himalaya brought forth more and more evidences suggestive of the presence of Early Man.

The studies of the lithic assemblage recovered from the Siwalik tract provided a consensus among scholars that the palaeolithic culture in NW Himalaya is distinguishable into two traditions, one based on pebble/cobble/boulder (Soanian culture) and other on flaked bifaces (Acheulain culture)[2]. Also that Soanian sites are widespread in the Siwalik tract whereas Acheulain sites are few and particularly confined only to the Potwar region (Pakistan). Recent excavations elsewhere in India has confirmed the co-existence of the two traditions in time and space.

Recent reports of palaeolithic artefacts in stratified context from parts of Potwar region, which are dated to 2 myr [3](Rendell and Dennell 1985), are geologically the oldest evidence of the existence of Early Man in Siwalik tract. In sharp contrast to the evidence from Pakistan, the sites so far reported from northwest India are on the terrace surface. Excepting a few flakes recovered from the loessic silt deposits, all other sites have hardly any stratigraphical context [4]. The techno-morphological characters and occurrence of artefacts on various terrace levels has been the basis for framing evolutionary and chronological pattern of the cultures [5]. Accordingly, the lithic assemblages from Jammu were classified into Early Soan, Late Soan, Final Soan and Neolithic in correspondence to the terrace surfaces [6].

The sites reported from Jammu Siwaliks are mostly located on the banks of ephemeral rivers, barring a few in close proximity to rivers Chenab and Tawi. Also these sites are situated in the plain zone of Siwalik range (most outer ranges of Siwalik), where rivers emerge out [7].

The discovery of a palaeolithic site near Katra is suggestive of the confirmatory evidence of the existence of Early Man in the deep and thickly forested Siwalik tracts. The site is about 3 km west of Katra town on Katra-Reasi highway (Fig. 1). It is located on the highest terrace surface on the right bank of river Banganga at the foot of Trikuta hills (Figs. 2 and 3). The terrace surface, presently under cultivation, perhaps was thickly vegetated as viewed from the present day physiographic condition in the surroundings. The top-soil (~ 50 cm) of the terrace surface (Fig. 4) have yielded the artefacts discussed herein. However, cultivation of the surface has caused the churning up of top-soil and the artefacts, therefore, have lost their primary context.

The collection of fifty artefacts from the site comprises both small and large sized artefacts. The small sized artefacts are made on vein quartzite whereas the larger ones are on compact sandstone. The small sized artefacts are essentially made on flakes and include types like, blade core, unfinished notch, end scrapers and side scrapers (Fig. 5). The collection of large sized artefacts is dominated by cores, followed by end scrapers and side scrapers. Essentially pebble/cobble size has been utilised in the preparation of large sized artefacts. Most of the artefacts preserve a part of cortex. The artefacts made out of compact sandstone are patinated and moderately abraded due to the sheet flow of the rain water on the terrace surface. Raw material is abundantly available in the surroundings. The quartz is easily available in the form of veins and plugs within limestone of Trikuta hills. The compact sandstone is extracted from the exposed outcrop of Lower Siwalik in the vicinity. The spread of the assemblage is limited to about 100 sq m of the widespread terrace surface. It is interesting to note that because of the non-availability of quartzite of pebble/cobble size, the fine-grained material has been used only for the preparation of small sized artefacts. The shaped artefacts of small size are finely retouched and in some cases have a defused bulb of percussion.

The terrace surface at Katra is a result of neotectonic activity during late Pleistocene [8]. The valley–fill deposits (Fig.4) caused by sudden uplift of Trikuta hills, underwent fluvial transportation and thus resulted in moderate sorting and bedding of the deposits during the period of quiescence. Subsequent to the formation of flat-topped (pseudo-terrace) surfaces, the area experienced subhumid to humid climatic conditions [9]. It is perhaps this environmental condition and availability of requisite geo-archaeological condition that the early man occupied the surface for habitation during the fag-end phase of Pleistocene, i.e. terminal Pleistocene) (~ 20,000 years before present).

It will not be an exaggeration to visualise the influx of the early man at Katra through the geographically and topographically contiguous Potwar region. There are evidences to substantiate the influx of the early man in Ladakh [10] and Nepal. These sites, on the basis of their small sizes, have been identified as shifting camps of the early man during transhumance.

Acknowledgments

The financial support provided by Head, PG Department of Geology, from the departmental field grant to conduct the field work is duly acknowledged by the authors.

Post-Graduate Department of Geology,
University of Jammu,
Jammu-180 004.

R.K. Ganjoo, Satish Safaya and Pankaj Lidoo

REFERENCES

1. De Terra, H. and T.T. Paterson. 1939. Study on the Ice Age in India and *Associated Cultures*, pp. 177-194. Washington: Carneige Publications.
2. Mohapatra, G.C. 1990. On the Track of Early Man in Western Sub-Himalaya, *Presidential Address, 77th Indian Science Congress*, Cochin.
3. Rendell, H.M. and R.W. Dennel. 1985. Dated Lower Palaeolithic Artefacts from Northern Pakistan, Current Anthropology, 26(3): 393.
4. De Terra, H. and Paterson, T.T. 1939. Op. cit.
5. Mohapatra, G.C. 1981. Environment and Culture of Early man in the Valley of Rivers Chenab and Ravi, Western Sub-Himalaya, *Proceedings X Congress of IUPPS, Mexico:* 90-123.
6. Saroj, H.M. 1974. Lithic Industries of Jammu. Unpublished Ph. D. Dissertation. Chandigarh: Panjab University.
8. Ganjoo, R.K. 1990. Late Pleistocene Fluvial Response to Tectonics in Jammu, *J & K, Journal of the Geological Society of India* 35 (4): 390-394.
7. Mohapatra, G.C. 1981. *Op. cit.*, Karir, B.S.1985. Gemorphology and Stone Age Culture of N.W. India, Delhi; Saroj, H.M. 1974. Op. cit
9. Ganjoo, R.K. 1993. Late Quaternary Climato-Tectonic History and Re-assessment of the Chronology of Prehistoric Cultures of Jammu Sub-Himalaya, India, in *Current Advances in Indian Archaeology Vol.. 1* (R.K. Ganjoo & S.B. Ota. Eds.), pp. 96-111 Nagpur: Dattsons.
10. Ota, S.B. 1993. Evidences of Transhumance from Ladakh Himalayas, Jammu & Kashmir, in *Current Advances in Indian Archaeology Vol. 1* (R.K. Ganjoo & S.B. Ota Eds.), 79-95. Nagpur: Dattsons.
11. Corvinus, G. 1990. A Note on the First Discovery of Handaxes in Nepal, Man and Environment XV (2): 9-12.

A Preliminary Report on the Faunal Remains at Paḍri : A Harappan Site in Bhavnagar District, Gujarat

Introduction

The ancient site of Padri is located in the Talaja Taluk of Bhavnagar District (Gujarat); the site is being excavated by the Deccan College Post-Graduate and Research Institute. This is a preliminary report on the bones collected from Padri during first two field seasons in 1990-91 and 1991-92. The site has revealed a twofold cultural sequence, i.e. Early Historic (Ist century B.C.-A.D.) and Harappan 3500–2000 B.C.).

Padri has yielded large quantities of animal remains (nearly 10000 in each season), which include bones, shells, ornaments and bone tools. The aim of this short report is to have a preliminary assessment of the bones before the complete quantum is examined. Thus this report is based on a random sample of a few bones from each lot, chosen and examined. It must be mentioned that the site has yielded a large number of shells and shell bangles. Both marine and freshwater molluscan shells have been bound at Padri. However, they have not been included here. The present report is based on bones collected from top layers 1-3 (Early Historic) and layer 4 (Harappan).

Animal Remains

A total of 200 bones were examined at the site itself. The material was found to be in fragmentary condition as observed in most of the Proto-historic sites in India. In some cases, a lot of substances were adhering to the bones and were hard to remove.

The bones after initial cleaning were identified with the help of modern collection of reference animal skeletons housed in the Deccan College. The bone sample revealed presence of five domestic and ten wild mammalian species. Besides, a large number of fish, crab and molluscs have been noticed, which will be examined later in detail. A list of mammals identified at Padri is given below.

Domestic	Wild
Bos Indicus (B.i)	*Boselaphus tragocamelus* (B.t)
Bubalus bubalis (B.b)	*Antilope cervicapra* (A.c)
Capra/Ovis (C/O)	*Axis axis* (A.a)
Sus domesticus (S.d)	*Sus scrofa* (S.s)
Canis familiaris (C.f)	*Canis aureus* (C.a)
	Canis lupus (C.l)
	Herpestes edwardsii (H.e)
	Bandicota indica (B.l)
	Lepus nigricollis (L.n)
	Rattus rattus (R.r)

A majority of the excavated archaeological sites in India has shown that the yield of, bones of domestic animals were several times more than that of wild animals. Among the domestic species, cattle accounted for 65% while sheep/goat contributed 6% of the Number of Identified Specimens (NISP–Table 5). Only one bone of domestic dog has been found in layer (3), which did not reveal any cut–mark (Table 3). It may have been brought by scavengers into the site and thus dog was not a part of the subsistence economy of Harappans at Padri.

The faunal diversity at Padri is interesting, since ten species of wild mammals could be identified. The wild mammals comprised of antelopes, chital, wild pig and carnivores like wolf and jackal. It is significant to note that the site has revealed presence of two species of rodents, viz. House rat and Bandicoot rat. These two animals contributed 8% of the total identifiable specimens (Table 5). The site at present shows many rat holes and thus their presence in the collection is not surprising.

The nilgai, blackbuck and chital have been represented by five bones each (2.5% of NISP) in the collection. At present, one can find several herds of nilgai near the site. However, blackbuck and chital are no longer found in the vicinity.

The site has yielded bones and shells in such a large quantity that they possibly outnumber other items. As the site is very near the sea–coast, the habitation might have been that of fishing community. The site has yielded some evidence of fish bones. However, the collection examined here is only a sample of hundreds of pieces. Thus it would be premature to comment on fishing activities at this stage.

The faunal assemblage suggests that the food economy of the people at Padri was possibly based on cattle pastoralism supported by some hunting in the nearby wilderness. Although a small sample has been studied, the exercise has opened a venue for future work and the range of possible interpretations that can be drawn from the faunal assemblage.

Acknowledgment

I express my thanks to the excavator Dr. V.S. Shinde and his team and also my colleague Ms. Seema Pawankar.

P.P. Joglekar

Dept. of Archaeology
Deccan College
Pune-411006

REFERENCES

1. Shinde, V.S., 1991 Excavations at Padri–1990-91: A Preliminary Report, Man and Environment 17 (1): 79-86.

Table 1
Skeletal Element Representation in Layer (1) at Padri

Bone	B.i	S.d	B.t	A.c
Scapula	01	–	–	01
Humerus	01	–	–	–
Pelvis	–	–	–	–
Astragalus	–	–	01	–
Vertebral	01	–	–	–
Ribs	01	–	–	–
Teeth	–	01	–	–
Upper Jaw Teeth	01	–	–	–
Total	07	01	01	01

Table 2
Skeletal Element Representation in layer (2) at Padri

Bone	B.i	B.b	C/O	S.d	B.t	A.c	A.a	H.e	L.n	R.r
Humerus	01	–	01	01	–	–	–	–	–	–
Radius	–	–	–	–	–	–	01	–	–	01
Ulna	01	–	–	01	–	–	–	–	–	–
Metacarpal	–	–	01	–	–	–	–	–	–	–
Femur	05	–	–	–	–	01	–	–	01	04
Tibia	04	–	–	–	–	–	–	–	–	01
Metatarsal	03	–	–	–	01	01	–	–	–	–

Pelvis	01	–	01	–	–	–	–	–	01	–
Astragalus	01	01	–	–	–	–	–	–	–	–
Calcaneum	04	–	–	–	–	01	–	–	–	–
Centrotarsal	01	–	–	–	–	–	–	–	–	–
Tarsal/Carpal	01	–	–	–	–	–	–	–	–	–
Phalanx I	03	01	01	–	–	–	–	–	–	–
Vertebral	05	–	–	–	–	–	–	–	–	–
Ribs	18	–	01	–	–	–	–	–	–	–
Teeth	02	–	–	–	–	–	–	01	–	01
Upper Jaw Teeth	03	–	01	–	–	–	–	–	–	–
Lower Jaw Teeth	03	–	–	–	–	–	–	–	–	–
Mandible	01	01	01	–	–	–	–	–	–	
Cranial	01	–	–	–	–	–	–	–	–	–
Total	57	03	05	02	01	03	01	01	02	07

Other Finds : Marine Fish Vertebrae 03

Table 3
Skeletal Element Representation in Layer (3) Padri

Bone	B.i	B.b	C/O	S.d	B.t	A.c	A.a	L.n	B.l	R.r
Scapula	03	–	01	–	–	–	–	–	–	–
Humerus	03	–	–	–	–	–	01	–	01	–
Radius	01	–	–	–	–	–	–	01	–	01
Ulna	01	–	–	–	–	–	–	–	–	–
Metatarsal	–	–	–	–	01	–	–	–	–	–
Pelvis	02	–	–	–	–	–	–	–	–	–
Fibula	–	–	–	–	–	–	–	–	–	–
Phalanx I	–	–	–	–	01	01	–	–	–	–
Phalanx II	01	–	–	–	–	–	–	–	–	–
Phalanx III	02	–	–	–	–	–	–	–	–	–
Vertebral	–	01	–	–	–	–	–	–	–	–
Ribs	14	–	01	–	–	–	–	–	–	–
Teeth	01	–	01	–	–	–	01	–	–	01
Upper Jaw Teeth	–	–	01	–	–	–	–	–	–	–
Lower Jaw Teeth	02	–	02	–	–	–	–	–	–	–
Maxilla	–	–	01	–	–	–	–	–	–	–
Total	33	01	06	01	02	01	02	01	01	07

Other Finds :	*Canis familiais*	01
	Canis lupus	01
	Canis aureus	01
	Marine Fish Vertebra	01

Table 4

Skeletal Element Representation in Layer (4) at Padri

Bone	B.i	B.b	C/O	B.t	A.a	S.s	C.l	B.l
Scapula	01	–	–	–	–	–	–	–
Humerus	01	–	–	–	–	–	01	–
Radius	02	–	–	–	–	–	–	–
Metacarpal	02	–	–	–	01	–	–	–
Femur	01	–	–	–	–	–	–	01
Metatarsal	02	02	–	01	–	–	–	–
Pelvis	01	–	–	–	–	–	–	–
Astragalus	03	–	–	–	–	–	–	–
Calcaneum	01	–	–	–	–	–	–	–
Phalanx I	03	–	01	–	–	–	–	–
Vertebral	02	–	–	–	–	–	–	–
Ribs	02	–	–	–	–	–	–	–
Teeth	–	–	–	–	01	–	–	–
Upper Jaw Teeth	02	–	–	–	–	–	–	–
Lower Jaw Teeth	–	–	–	–	–	–	–	–
Maxilla	01	–	–	–	–	01	–	–
Mandible	–	–	01	–	–	01	–	–
Total	33	02	02	01	02	01	01	01

Other Finds : Freshwater Crab 02

Fish 01

Table 5

Number of Identified Specimens (NISP) at Padri

Species	(1)	(2)	(3)	(4)	Total	%NISP
Bos indicus	7	57	33	33	130	65.00
Bubalus bubalis	–	3	1	2	6	3.00
Capra/Ovis	–	5	6	2	13	6.50
Sus domesticus	1	2	1	–	4	2.00
Canis familiaris	–	–	1	–	1	0.50
Boselaphus tragocamelus	1	1	2	1	5	2.50
Antilope cervicapra	1	3	1	–	5	2.50
Axis axis	–	1	2	2	5	2.50
Sus scrofa	–	–	1	–	1	0.50

Canis aureus	–	–	1	–	1	0.50
Canis lupus	–	–	1	1	2	1.00
Herpestes edwardsii	–	1	–	–	1	0.50
Bandicota indica	–	–	1	1	2	1.00
Lepus nigricollis	–	2	1	–	3	1.50
Rattus rattus	–	7	7	–	14	7.00
Fish	–	3	1	1	5	2.50
Crab	–	–	–	2	2	1.00
Total	10	85	59	46	200	100.20

Excavation of Tisseru Stupa (Ladakh)

Ladakh, known in Tibetan as La-tags 'land of many passes', is a mountainous border area on the north of the country. It covers approximately an area of 100,000 square km and lies between the two highest mountain ranges of the world, i.e. the Himalaya in the south and the Karakoram in the north. It is bounded on the northeast by the Kuenlun ranges, on the east and south by the Chinese districts of Rudok and Chumurti, on the extreme south by Lahul and Spiti valley and on the west by Khurmang, Chorbat and the areas of Askardu. It is divided into five regions: Leh, Nubra, Rupshu, Zanskar and lower Ladakh. Leh is the administrative headquarters of Ladakh and is situated in the big flat valley of the Indus river. Nubra falls on the north and north eastern side. The lower Ladakh lies along the road which joins Ladakh with the Kashmir valley. The principal river of the region is Indus which flows from southeast to northwest through the greater part of the region. A number of smaller tributaries also join it, amongst which Shyok on the north, Zanskar, Suru and Drass on the south are important.

It is said that in summer Leh, the chief town and headquarters of Ladakh, was the meeting place of travellers. The earliest authentic references to Ladakh are from the records of the Chinese pilgrims, Fa-hien, Hieun Tsang and others. Fa-Hien visited Ladakh in A.D. 399–400 and called it Kie-cha. Fa-Hein records that he saw the king of the country holding *Pancha Parishad*, the great quinquennial assembly first instituted by Emperor Asoka for general confession of sins and inculcation of morality. He also mentions that two relics of Buddha – one of them was a spittoon made of stone, and another a tooth over which a *stupa* was erected, which has not yet been properly identified. Heiun-Tsang mentions Ladakh under a new name-Mo-lo-po. Approximately at this time, 7th cent. A.D. The western part of Leh town was inhabitated by the descendants of Dards.

Cunningham in his *Ancient Geography of India* says that the area on western bank of the River Indus was occupied by Dards, who were nomads coming from Central Tibet to the plains and foot-hills of Ladakh to graze their cattle along the Indus. Their graves have been located near a stupa, locally known as Tisseru.

Francke excavated a few graves in the early twenties and salvaged a few antiquities, thus establishing the antiquity of Dardic people in the Ladakh region. He described the Tisseru stupa in his report casually but did not pay much attention to its antiquity and tradition revolving round it.

Tisseru stupa is located nearly 4 km to the north west of Leh city, amidst cultivated fields. On the west of it extensive sandy slopes form the background and on the east cultivated terraces provide lush green environment in summer; in the winter dry snow covers the area. Tisseru stupa or Teu-gser-po derives its name from *Teu* (Mule) *Iser-po* = yellow rock (mule-shaped yellow rock) and it was believed that there used to live an evil spirit in the cavity of the rock which was troubling the inhabitants of Leh. The lower portion of this rock is visible from the southeast side of the lowest terrace of the stupa. To exorcise its evil effect, King Bum-Ide erected a stupa to cover up the rock. On account of this it is also known as Teu-Ta-Shils, i.e. Brilliant good fortune.

The stupa is partly buried and partly exposed. It is nearly 25m in height and is built in several terraces. The lowest terrace is circular with a circumference of 174.74 m followed by another circular terrace with a circumference of 152.74m and with a depth of 3.50m. and again followed by a square terrace. Above the square terrace are receding square walls of the stupa which appears to be circular on top. On the top terrace sun-dried bricks of size 11 × 12 × 44 cm and 10 × 2 × 40 cm have been used. Rubble stones are also used in the top portion of the stupa.

To know the full sequence and extent of the structure, scientific clearance was started in 1981 and a portion of the stupa was exposed. A clear picture of the structures could not be obtained at that time as the working season was short and temperature went down to minus 10 degree Celcius. Again in the year 1986 regular excavations were planned and continued for three sucessive seasons, i.e. 1986 to 1988. Since Leh is situated 11500ft. above MSL the working season is always limited and at times dry cold sand laden winds also create an unhealthy atmosphere. Under such difficult weather conditions appreciable results were achieved which are summarised here.

To facilitate easy working and to obtain an accurate picture of this highly damaged structure the whole structure was divided into grids to lay bare several levels and also to ascertain details of chapels built inside the stupa. As the digging earlier to 1986 was confined to the eastern side, the present excavations were carried out on the northern and other sides. The northern side was a highly damaged one; it appeared that sometimes in the past either due to some fault in the construction or natural calamity a major portion of the upper structures had the fallen down and buried the lower terraces. From the top gradually and very carefully fallen debris was removed. The remnants of the topmost structure distinctly indicated its once being square in plan over which a circular structure was built partly of stone and partly of sun dried mud bricks. The excavations further revealed an entrance in the middle of the circular structure. The entrance was supported by wooden beams and poles. It was also flanked by small vaults built of stones on either side.

The excavations in the lower grids revealed traces of rock-surfaces over which the stupa was raised. It appeared that the rock surface was used as a solid base and foundation for the structure. Over the uneven rock base rubble structure was built in the form of circular construction which served the purpose of first circular terrace. This lowest or first circular terrace is 3 to 340m deep and 0.80 to 3.00m. high. Above the lowest terrace traces of upper circular terrace were encountered. This upper terrace is 4m in height. Above these two circular terraces the remains of four successive walls with a gap of 0.50 to 0.70m in ascending order were encountered. The gap between the walls appeared to be a passage through abutting walls. The lower portions of walls are built with rubble stones and the upper portions with sun-dried bricks. The lower and outermost wall is supported by a buttress wall which runs all around the structure.

Besides, traces of a doorway were also noticed on the northeast corner. The interesting aspect of the circular terraces was the evidence of mud plaster over the rubble wall and stucco decoration.

During the course of excavation a large number of painted fragments were found. It is difficult to ascertain at what level and on what surface the murals were executed. In one such fragment hand gesture *(mudra)* was noticed which indicated that the stupa was decorated with human figures. The colours used are vermilion, ultramarine, green, white, cobalt blue and brilliant red. Lines are, however, executed in black. Besides, a large number of clay tablets depicting Buddhist deities such as Sakyamuni, Manjusri, Tara, Samvara, votive stupa in relief and a manuscript written in golden colour are noteworthy, though fragile in condition. These tablets are of sun-dried soft clay.

Exposing this gigantic stupa and the explorations in Ladakh revealed for the first time that the stupa in the Himalayan region were built generally on natural contours; the lower portions were built in stone and the upper ones with mud bricks. The structures were plastered with locally available clay and the plastered portions were decorated with paintings depicting mythological scenes. In the body of structures, clay tablets were kept inside the core depicting different Buddhist divinities.

Superintending Archaeologist,
Archaeological survey of India Bhopal Circle, Bhopal.

R.C. AGRAWAL

Anangpur Fort: The Earlier Tomar Settlement Near Delhi

The fort of Anangpur (28° 27' 40"N, 77° 15' 30"E) in Distt. Faridabad, Haryana, is located towards west of the village of the same name. In its vicinity is a hillock. On its eastern slopes is located the old habitational area. It has, however, considerably increased in the present century along with hundreds of modern constructions all around. The village Anangpur is situated some 30 km south of Delhi and 5 km southwest of Surajkund. The region is the quartzite tableland of the Aravallis in its Tuglaqabad Gurgaon stretch, with an average height of about 243 m above mean sea level.

Although the fort was noticed by Carr Stephen (1876) in the last century, and also by other archaeologists, yct neither any details were recorded by them nor any description was published even in the subsequent period when serious archaeological investigations were undertaken in the area. Archaeologists, it may be noted were primarily interested in the Surajkund and Anangpur dam located in the vicinity; these were declared as 'protected monuments' by the Archaeological Survey of India in the beginning of the present century.

A palaeolithic site, located towards the south of Anangpur village, was discovered in 1986. Subsequently extensive explorations were undertaken in the area in 1991 and 1992 by the Prehistory Branch of the Archaeological Survey of India under A.K. Sharma and S.B. Ota. (Sharma & Ota 1991) A few trenches were laid at different places in order to ascertain the position of implementiferous horizon and a large number of late Acheulian tools of quartzite, comprising of handaxes, cleavers, scrapers, points, discoids, etc. were found both in the excavations and in surface collections. The area was also explored by the author, from the Delhi Circle of A.S.I, and Sri Ram Saran, the second author, from the Excavation Branch II of the Archaeological Survey of India. During exploration hundreds of palaeolithic tools were collected. In December 1992 the village area and adjoining hillock with the remains of ancient fortifications and structures of its citadel were explored by the authors and Sri Ram Saran along with their teams.

Anangpur, also called Anekpur or Arangpur, was inhabited by Anang Pal of the Tomar dynasty. There were definitely two and possibly three rulers of the same name in the dynastic history of the Tomars. Anang Pal II constructed the Lal Kot and inhabited the first city of Delhi in between A.D 1052 to 1060. (Cunningham 1871; Mani 1991. Thus, it seems that Anangpur was either founded by Anang Pal II, or if earlier than him, then most probably by Anang Pal I. Cunningham (1871) has cited the opinion of Sir Syed Ahmed about the foundation of Anangpur in Samvat 733 (A.D. 676) by Anang Pal I, but according to him the above date seems to be in the Valabhi era of A.D 318. Thus the foundation of Anangpur, as per his view seems to have taken place in A.D. 1051 by Anang Pal II who also founded Delhi in the same year. According to one recent view the date of Anang Pal I ranges from A.D. 736 to 754 (Dwivedi 1973).

The exploratory survey of the site and the study of architectural features do not help much to arrive at a definite conclusion about the date of the construction of the fort and the period of its occupation in the 7th-8th century or 11th century A.D. As the data collected are quite insufficient archaeological excavation of the fort alone would shed some light on this otherwise a comparatively dark chapter of the Rajput history of Delhi and its neighbourhood. Since Anang Pal II constructed Lal Kot and peopled Delhi in the middle of the 11th century A.D., the question arises about the location of the habitation and the seat of administration of the Tomar rulers of Delhi who preceded Anang Pal II. It is, therefore, quite logical and traditionally accepted that the Tomars, who had the status of feudatory rulers under the Pratiharas in the beginning had settled, in the Aravallis, most probably at Anangpur, in the 8th century and continued there till they became fully independent rulers in the 11th century A.D. It is then that they shifted their royal seat to Lal Kot and founded a new city, called Ḍhilī, Ḍhillikā or Ḍhillikāpurī. It was done in the erstwhile temple township of Yoginīpura, where they had constructed a number of temples, the ruined architectural fragments of which are scattered in the Qutb Archaeological Area and in its vicinity.

Among the two major Tomar Rajput monuments of the area, the Anangpur dam was definitely constructed to block the upstream rain-water for irrigation of the fields. About 50 metres wide and 7 metres high dam with sluice, or trap-doors, at its openings for controlled flow of water in the ravine, is a well known architectural marvel of the period. A number of ravines in the hilly parts of the area terminated as different palaeochannels of Yamuna, the last of which is the fifth palaeochannel which flowed in prehistoric times through Surajkund area towards the northeast of Anangpur dam. Taking advantage of the connecting internal drainage system and the depression of the palaeochannel the Tomars had constructed Surajkund, a reservoir with stepped stone embankment on a semicircular plan.

During the course of exploration of the area in 1992, a Nagari inscription (P1.I) written in 5 lines within a square frame on an upright quartzite stone block, standing vertically in the fields, was found. It mentions probably some year (Saṁvat 1618) and numerals, not easily legible. The lower part of a stone sculpture (P1.II) of 9th-10th, century showing a seated drummer to the left of the main broken figure was the only other antiquarian remain noticed in the lower area of the hill in the village.

The fort wall, covered under debris on the western side of the village, gradually rises from the southern slopes of the hillock and runs towards north with varying thickness, between 3 to 4 metres covering the crest of the hill from south, west and north sides. The length of the elliptical fort wall (P1.III) is more than 300 metres in north-south orientation and traces of 21 semicircular bastions were noticed all along the wall, each located at an interval of 15 to 16 metres (fig. 1). The rampart and bastions were constructed with local worked stone blocks of large and medium sizes. In the middle of the wall a gap of about 4 metres was noticed in between two bastions which perhaps represents the western gateway of the fort. Some constructions of rubble structures with thick lime-plaster were noticed abutting to the southwestern part of one of the bastions. Southern and western sides of the fort-wall overlook a deep gorge caused by heavy waterflow during the rainy season, which seemingly served the purpose of the ditch around the fort. The area of northern and eastern sides of the fort is formed on a gradual slope of the hill down below which the village of Anangpur is situated. Because of the habitational activities of the village, traces of eastern and northern walls of the fort are not visible on the surface.

The two mounds, on the crest of the hillock within the fortification, one at the northern end and the other at the southern end, appear like watchposts. A few paleolithic stone tools were found there. Outlines of some of the constructions, including streets and chambers, near the only extant western gateway of the fort, were also observed. A circular copper coin was found at this spot which is definitely of Rajput origin. It has on obverse a crude representation, possibly, of Śiva with bull, and traces of Nāgarī legend on reverse. It seems to be an early Tomar coin type. Red ware potsherds of medium to coarse fabric comprising of storage jars, lids, cooking pots, basins, bowls, etc. are found in this (citadel) area of the fort. The absence of glazed ware at the site suggests the site to be a single-culture site of the Rajput period, bracketed between the 8th and 11th century A.D.

It has been surmised (Dwivedi 1973 : 189), on the basis of *Kuṭṭanīmata* written by Dāmodaragupta, the Prime Minister of Vinayāditya Jayāpīda (c. A.D.779-813), the ruler of Kashmir, that the area of the Kurus was also called Anaṅga Pradeśa. Possibly, therefore, Harshavardhana, who ruled from Thanesar, was called Anaṅga-Harsha– "devanikctanamanaṅga Harshe gate tridivalokam....."

Various legends and genealogical lists give the name of the first ruler of the Tomar dynasty as Vilhaṇadeva, Bilandeva, Jājū or Jāula who seems to have acquired the title of Anaṅgapāla when he became the ruler of this area and became famous in history as Anang Pal I.

A number of Sanskrit texts on Śilpa-Śāstra mention the types and planning of forts. The Anangpur fort comes under the category of *giri-durga* or hill fort. About the planning of hill-forts, which can be located on the crest of the hill or in the middle of the hills or near the hill (*Mānasāra* - Durganiveśanam-46; Viśvakarmā Vāstuśāstra-dvādaś adurgavidhiḥ-3), the *Nāradaśilpśāstra* (Pañchavidhadurganirmāṇakrama-Kathanam-7) gives the details. It includes walls, gateways, watchposts, ditch, streets, palaces, temples, residences of nobles and generals and storage of treasury and other items. In Chapter 45 (Durga-prākārakalpanam-40) of *Samarāṅgaṇa Sūtradhāar* the hillforts have been described as the best among various categories of forts–"Sarveshāmeva durgāṇām Pārvatīyam praśasyate". The *Viśvakarmā Vāstuśāstra* (dvādaśadurgavidhiḥ–4-5), while giving details of structures in a hill-fort, mentions about its facing which is towards the east or north side.

"Madhyasthadevaprāsādam devamandirabhūshitam

Mantryadiparivārāṇām bhavanādyaissamanvitam

Prāchīmukam prakartavyamathavottaradiṁmukham

Bhaṭaiḥ Khadgadharairanyaissamantātsaṁvṛtāṅgaṇam".

The location of structures at the crest of the Anangpur fort on the eastern side, and the orientation of the fort and the streets in its citadel from north to south suggest that it faced east, overlooking the valley in its front, where a township flourished with rich agricultural fields in the midst of the Aravalli ranges. Further excavations will definitely throw important light on the architecture and archaeology of the area which may help in reconstructing the missing-links of the Tomar history of the region as well as the prehistoric past of the entire region.

Archaeological Survey of India,
New Delhi.

B.R. Mani
I.D. Dwivedi

REFERENCES

1. Stephen, Carr. 1876 *The Archaeology And Monumental Remains of Delhi*,
2. Sharma, A.K. and S.B.Ota 1991 'Anangpur: A Palaeolithic Site near Delhi', *Puratattva*, 21, 1990-91, pp. 74-75. Also 'The Palaeolithic Site Near Delhi' New Trends in Indian Art and Archaeology - *S.R. Rao's 70th Birthday Felicitation Volume*, Delhi, 1991 pp.1-13.
3. Mani B.R. 1992 'Excavations at Lal Kot 1991-92 and further Explorations in Delhi'. *Puratattva*, No. 22, 1991-92, p.75.
4. Cunningham, A. 1871 B,R, *Archaeological Survey of India-Four Reports Made During the years 1862-63-64-65*, Delhi, 1871, p.151. Also Dwivedi, Harihar Niwas, Dilli Ke Tomar. (Hindi), Gwalior, 1973. P.191.
5. Cunningham, Jbid p.152
6. Dwivedi, Harihar Niwas.1973 *Dilli Ke Tomar*. (Hindi) Gwalior, p. 191.

   Mani, B.R. 1991. 'Citadel of Lal Kot, Delhi', Pragdhara, Journal of the U.P. State Archaeological Organisation, 1991-92, pp. 147-50.

A Report on IOC Organised National Conference on Pollution and Historical Monuments

The Indian Oil Corporation Limited organised a 2-day National Conference on 'Environmental Pollution and Preservation of Historical Monuments' on 31st October and 1st November, 1994 in New Delhi. This conference was in pursuit of their mission for preservation of 'ecological balance and national heritage' with the main aim to deliberate on the issues related to deterioration of historical monuments and sensitise opinion for evolving an integrated approach towards formulation of environmental management and preservation strategies for these objects of our rich Culture heritage. More than 100 experts representing different scientific disciplines and Institutions numbering about 30, participated in the Conference.

The 2-day Conference was divided into six technical sessions dealing with ambient air quality standards, pollution management of historical sites, meteorological parameters, vegetation as pollution-sink, effect of pollution on monuments and air pollution and Taj. The scientific papers presented in different sessions were 29 in numbers.

It was inaugurated by the IOC management and keynote address was given by Dr. D. K. Biswas, Chairman, CPCB who hailed the mission of IOC for taking steps to preserve the ecological balance and national heritage. In the introductory session, Shri K. N. Dikshit discussed the 'Cultural heritage of India with reference to historical monuments', whereas Shri S. S. Saini gave an idea about 'Environmental management practices at Mathura refinery', including the need for conservation of environment through minimising the emissions from refinery. Dr. B. Sengupta discussed the 'Ambient air quality standards'. In the next session, Prof D. P. Kambo, Shri R. Sengupta, Ms Padma S. Rao and Dr. Rekha Thakre presented their papers on 'Pollution management of Historic Sites', whereas Dr. M. M. Lal, Dr. V. M. Sharma and Shri H. O. Gupta and S. K. Singh discussed 'Causes of deterioration and protective measures,' 'Geotechnical environmetal aspects' and 'Physio-chemical requirements', respectively. Dr V. M. Sharma was of opinion that there is a need to monitor the safety of monuments by adequate instrumentation. Shri B. B. Chakravorty circulated a paper on 'Environmental management at Indian oil Refineries' and informed that adoption of environmentally sound and sustainable development practice is an integral part of the Corporate philosophy of IOC.

In session III, Dr. B. Padmanabhamurty and K. C. Sahoo discussed from the meteorological approach 'Impact of industrial emissions on air quality at Agra and Bharatpur', wheras Dr. Maithili Sharan explained the 'Use of dispersion models for finding impact on air quality'. Dr. Manju Mohan dealt on 'Elevated stacks'. In the next session Prof. M. M. Bhandari spoke on the 'Role of plants in Nullifying Air Pollution' and was of opinion that it is imperative to have a proper understanding of plant response and pollutant concentration relationship with environmental conditions. Prof. Jaweed Ashraf outlined the 'Vegetation in mediaeval cities' with reference to ecological conditions of mediaeval Agra, whereas Dr. Sashi Dhawan stressed in her paper that plants are self-renewing and can act as persitant absorbers of pollutants.

In session V, Dr. O. P. Agrawal Dr M. C. Ganorkar, Dr. B. B. Lal, Dr. J. K. Moitra, Dr. B. Sengupta and Dr. S. P. Singh spoke on the 'Effect of pollution and other factors on monuments'. Dr. Agrawal while dealing with the deterioration and conservation of stone monuments suggested a multi-disciplinary approach, whereas Dr. B. B. Lal was of the view that monuments have deteriorated on account of general chemical weathering, aging and physical disintegration. Dr. M. C. Ganorkar talked on 'A new aproach to protect historical buildings made of marble stones', and suggested that some organic compounds developed by him can be employed for preservation purposes. Dr. J. K. Moitra in his paper suggested monitoring and analysis procedure to determine the deterioration of monuments. Prof. Jaweed Ashraf from the 'Experience' of Sun Temple at Konark' brought-forth humidity and light as a great damaging factor. Dr. Shashi Dhawan discussed the problem of 'Bio-deterioration of Monuments and Buildings'. The environmental conditions permit the growth of organisms and this could be treated by a number of chemicals.

The last session was devoted to Air-Pollution and Taj. Shri B. N. Tandon suggested monitoring of concentration of gaseous pollutants (SO2, NO_x), whereas Dr. B. B. Lal mentioned that the acidic gases from the industry may not cause any corrosion of the stone or sulphation problem but a perceptible discolouration is seen on some parts of mausoleum. This may be due to the deposition of fine dust and smoke particles, emanating partly from the emissions of the industry and partly from the dust-laden winds. Shri H. O. Gupta in his paper on Aerometric surveillance' presented the ambient air quality data monitored at the Taj Mahal in respect of dust-fall measurement and suspended particulate matter. Dr. M. Aslam stressed the need on 'Conserving the architectural heritage' through public awareness. IOC also circulated a paper on 'A journey of sulphur oxides in atmosphere'.

In the concluding session thrust areas were identified and followng recommendations were made.

1. Integrated and comprehensive study be made to assess the impact of environmental pollution and other natural factors on monuments of historical importance and to find the causes for deterioration to seek long-term remedial measures.

2. Monitoring of atmospheric pollutants and meteorological parameters should be carried out at the places of Natural Heritage and long-term data base be developed.

3. Scientific approach is required to develop green-belt around monuments as an effective pollution abatement measure.

4. Central Govt. to appoint a National Committee to integrate the efforts of various agencies involved in conservation of national heritage. IOC will form a care committee in collaboration with others for steering the initial efforts.

5. Support of major industries in preserving historical monuments and creating mass awareness programmes.

Some of the important environmental issues which continue to haunt Indian environmentalists and conservators were discussed in detail. However, it was noticed that in the absence of financial support and meagre allotment of funds for preservation of monuments by Govt., not much progress has been made. The Institutions identified by the Varadrajan Committee have yet to start their work for ascertaining the present status of the monuments and also suggest air-pollution control technology.

This conference which was arranged by the IOC., was a great success in bringing together eminent experts of different disciplines for experience sharing and bringing out the above action areas. It is hoped that IOC shall continue such efforts in future also. The IOC management specially Shri B.B. Chakravorty of Safety and Environment Protection department deserves all praise for sucessfully organising this conference and also for their desire to adopt the latest available technology for pollution monitroing and control.

INDIAN ARCHAEOLOGICAL SOCIETY.

BOOK REVIEWS

Shiv Kumar Sharma, *Painted Scrolls of Asia*, (Hindu, Buddhist and Lamaist) Intellectual Publishing House, Delhi, pp. 116, Plates 87, Price Rs. 450/-

Scrolls paintings are the older versions of our present-day coloured films such as the Ramayana and the Mahabharat. These are done on cloth or paper, or even leather and hemp cloth and are found in north-eastern India, Nepal, Bangladesh, Sri Lanka, Thailand, Indonesia, Tibet, China, Mongolia, Chinese Central Asia, Bhutan etc. i.e. primarily in those countries where Buddhism has been and is still a popular religion although Krishna and Rama legends were also portrayed in eastern Indian states, as well as Indonesia for the Vaishnavites.

The paintings had narrations of the stories connected with the life of the Buddha or else the Jataka stories. The episodes were arranged in successive panels arranged vertically one above the other. The wandering monks narrated the stories verbally and also made them rich visually through the scroll paintings realising the fact that what is visually presented particularly to the illiterate masses of those ancient days gets easily and permanently registered in the mind. Stone monuments created the institution of pilgrimage and it could be undertaken by the lay-disciples hardly once in life-time but what about the other times and what about those who are unable to undertake hazardous journeys? For all these people the scroll paintings proved a boon. We have the actual remains of such scroll paintings from the 7th-8th century A.D. caves of Dun-Huang in Chinese Central Asia.

Dr. Sharma's book lavishly illustrated with coloured and black-and-white plates is second in the series. It deals with the scroll paintings of all the countries and regions mentioned above. It has taken into account not only the technical aspects of the paintings and the themes of the painted narratives but also the aesthetic appreciation of the paintings. Prof. G.C. Pande, world's one of the most renowned scholars of Buddhism, has enhanced the utility of the book by his Foreword to the book.

It is a beautifuly printed and produced book and will be useful to scholars of Buddhism and Buddhist art.

S.P. Gupta

Vijay Kumar Malhotra, Kamal-Śāśvata Sānskratika Pratīka (Hindi), Praveen Parkashan, Delhi-110030, pp. 300, Plates 150 Colour 13.

Here is a book by a distinguished Hindi writer, and incidentally a Member of Parliament from Delhi. A life-long teacher of Hindi literataure in Delhi University, Dr. Malhotra worked very hard even in the extremely difficult disciplines of Tantras, Mantras, Symbolism, Hindu Iconography, Buddhist and Jain philosophies as well as their art and architecture besides his own discipline of Hindi literataure. Here is, therefore, a mine of information on a single, seemingly very small, subject-the flower lotus, the seat of all our gods and goddesses.

The author has gone deep into the subject and looked at lotus from various angles – both sacred and profane. The selection of photographs from ancient and contemporary art and architecture, over 150, to illustrate the subject, has been well thought of.

No one interested in the subject of lotus in art and literature can easily afford to miss it.

Printed and produced completely on imported art paper from a very distinguished printing house in Delhi, it is a model of publication, particularly in Hindi.

S.P. Gupta

Pradhan, Shail, *Bhārtīya Kalā me Vaishṇava Paramparā*, (Hindi) National Centre for Oriental Studies, Delhi, 1992, pp. 183, Price Rs. 350/-

The present book is a revised Ph.D. thesis of the author. Divided into eight chapters, the author has brought forth the development of Vaishnav cult from 320 A.D. to 1250 A.D. The main aim of the work was to highlight the Vaishnavite figurines kept in the different museums of Madhya Pradesh. Starting from the historical and religious background, the author has discussed the origin and development of Vaishṇavism and also referred to the important centres of Vaishṇava activities. She has also made a survey of Vaishṇava cults and classified them from iconographic angle. The details of ornaments and other aspects of culture have also been discussed for comparison.

This book which is in chaste Hindi is specially valuable for those students who are interested in the sculptural art of India.

K.N. Dikshit

Sudhir Kumar Trivedi, *Madhya Bharat Ki Pratihara Kalina Kala tatha Sthapatya* (Hindi) (Publications Scheme, Jaipur 1994) pp.158 + 20, Plates 63, Plans and Elevations of Temples 8, Price Rs. 750/-

Here is a book written exclusively on the art and architecture of Pratiharas in Madhya Bharat, broadly northern Madhya Pradesh, in Hindi, in a large format. The subject is old and several attempts have been made in the past to deal with the Pratihara temples in M.P. but rarely in-depth study based upon thorough field-work in a comparatively limited geographical area was made and published in the national language of India. And also rarely 9" × 11" format was adopted by Hindi publishers giving large photographs on very good art paper where one can see all details.

The book, a revised version of the Ph.D. thesis of the author, has six chapters-Political History, Temple Architecture, Iconography, Sculpture, Epigraphs and Seals and Conclusions, plus the usual Bibliography, Index, etc. Chapter I is based upon the explorations conducted by the author, hence quite informative for future scholars of the subject since several additions have been made to our knowledge, atleast in details. The chapter on sculpture is also informative though some of the iconographic identifications will remain highly controversial, for example, Plate 47, a bronze from National Museum identified as Hayagriva is not correct since Vishnu's face is not that of the horse. Similarly, we fail to understand as to why the female deity on owl (Plate 53) be called 'Chamunda' when iconography of the deity is not at all suggestive of this identification. The details of secondary images are, however, quite informative. The chapter on epigraphs is quite useful and so also the conclusions.

Printed on very good paper, neatly and celarly, the book will be useful for everyone.

Shashi Asthana

INDEX TO PURĀTATTVA
Nos. 1 to 23

Purnima Ray *

The Index has two divisions—Author and Title.

Names of Authors, articles, notes/news, miscellaneous items are arranged alphabetically, followed by the Title, Purātattva no., Year and Page no., e.g. Asthana, Shashi. Dynamics of Pre-Harappan Cultures. 13 & 14, 1981-83, pp. 45-50.

The Title part has all the titles of articles, notes, news, miscellaneous items arranged under their titles alphabetically followed by the names of respective contributors, Purātattva, Year and Page no., e.g. Recent Advances in the Study of the Indus Script. Iravatham Mahadevan. 9, 1977-78, pp. 34-42.

AUTHOR INDEX

Agrawal, D.P.
Genesis of Harappa Culture. 6, 1972-73, pp. 37-41.

Indian Civilization: The Formative Period. Indian Institute of Advanced Studies, Simla, 1968; 4, 1970-71, pp. 63-65.

Metal Technology of the Indian Protohistoric Cultures: Its Archaeological Implications. 3, 1969-70, pp. 15–22.

Protohistoric Chronology and Technology, and Ecological Factors: A Synthesis. 1, 1967-68, pp. 17-23.

Session On NBP. 5, 1971-72, pp. 34-35.

Session on OCP. 5, 1971-72, pp. 9-10.

— and **Kusumgar, Sheela**
On the Calibration of C^{14} Dates. 7, 1974, pp. 70-73.

— and **Margabandhu, C.**
Ancient Gold Working: Some New ^{14}C Dates. 8, 1975-76, pp. 138-139.

Agrawal, O.P.
Atmospheric Pollution and Cultural Property. 13 & 14, 1981-83, pp. 149-154.

Taj Mahal — Some Issues of Conservation. 23, 1992-93, pp. 40-47.

— and **Harinarain, Bhatia, S.K.**
Technical Studies of Iron implements from the Megalithic Site Tadakanahalli. 12, 1980-81, pp. 97-100.

— and **Jain, Kamal K. Singh, Tej**
Technical Examination of Some Medieval Glazed Wares from Fatehpur Sikri. 17, 1986-87, pp. 50-53.

— and **Sharma, V.C.**
Note on the Treatment of an excavated Iron Object. 11, 1979-80, pp. 159-160.

Agrawala, P.K.
Note on the Antiquity of Seal. 8, 1975-76, p. 141.

* Library & Information Assistant
Archaeological Survey of India
Delhi Circle, New Delhi

Prehistoric Bronze Anthropomorph in the Patna Museum and Its Identification. 1, 1967-68, pp. 96-98.

Three Crystal Pendants of Identical Design. 2, 1968-69, pp. 49-50.

Two Relic Caskets from Mathura. 3, 1969-70, pp. 49-52.

Agrawala, R.C.
Chaturmukha Śiva-linga from Nand, near Pushkar, Rajasthan. 2, 1968-69, pp. 53-54.

Ahmad, Nisar
Stratigraphy, Probable Climatic Phases and Dating of the Stone Age Cultures of Upper Son Valley. 2, 1968-69, pp. 41-45.

Two Early Stone Age Sites on River Son in District Bilaspur, M.P. 1, 1967-68, pp. 87-89.

Anon.
Braj Basi Lal. 13 & 14, 1981-83, vii & viii.

Akhtar, Jamna Das
Indo-Aryan Rulers of Ancient Western Asia and Their Documents. 10, 1978-79, pp. 66-69.

Asia Week, Hong Kong
Saving a Great Asian Empire. 22, 1991-92, pp. 139-140.

Asthana, Shashi
Dynamics of Pre-Harappan Culture. 13 & 14, 1981-83, pp. 45-50.

Mahāparinirvāṇa Panel in the National Museum Collection. 16, 1985-86, pp. 35-37.

Rakta-Lokeśvara in Indian Buddhist Art. 19, 1988-89, pp. 43-45.

Rare Image of Avalokiteśvara from Eastern India. 20, 1989-90, pp. 113-114.

Unique Pātravāhaka Yaksha Image from Ahichchhatra. 11, 1979-80, pp. 74-77.

Atre, Shubhangana
Lady of Beasts–The Harappan Goddess. 16, 1985-86, pp. 7-13.

Badam, G.L.
Pleistocene Fossil Vertebrates in India. 13 & 14, 1981-83, pp. 123-137.

Bajpei, K.D.
Harappan and Vedic Civilization: An Analysis of Legacy. 20, 1991-92, pp. 115-117.

Location of Pāvā. 16, 1985-86, pp. 76-78.

Rāmāyaṇa: Some Problems Re-examined. 10, 1978-79, pp. 76-78.

University of Saugar (Archaeology in Universities Series). 2, 1968-69, pp. 63-64.

Vaṅga and Vāhlika. 17, 1986-87, pp. 26-30.

Banerjee, N.R.
Comments on the 'Concept of Urban Revolution'. 6, 1972-73, pp. 32-33.

Outlines of the Archaeology of Nepal. 2, 1968-69, pp. 1-10.

Session on OCP. 5, 1971-72, p.15.

Banerjee, S.
Archaeological Material from West Bengal in the Zoological Survey of India. 11, 1979-80, pp. 162-164.

Banerjee, Tulika
Typological Differences Between Indian and European Upper Palaeolithic Assemblages. 12, 1980-81, pp. 113-114.

Behera, Pradip K.
Sulabhdihi: A Neolithic Celt Manufacturing Centre in Orissa. 22, 1991-92, pp. 124-132.

Bhan, Kuldeep K. and Kenoyer, J.M.
Nageshwar, an Industrial Centre of Chalcolithic Period. 12, 1980-81, pp. 115-120.

Bhan, Suraj
Session on OCP. 5, 1971-72, pp. 16-21.

Siswal: A Pre-Harappan Site in Drishadvati Valley. 5, 1971-72, pp. 44-46.

Bhardwaj, H.C.
Abstract from 'Some Technical Observations on NBP Ware Slip', in "Potteries in Ancient India". 5, 1971-72, pp. 62-63.

Copper Red Glasses Through the Ages. 3, 1969-70, pp. 2-8.

Note on the Chemical Composition of Some Glass Beads from Rajghat, Varanasi. 1, 1967-68, pp. 42-46.

Rajghat Copper–A Metallurgical View. 2, 1968-69, pp. 30-34.

Studies in Ancient Indian Technology: A Review. 13 & 14, 1981-83, pp. 139-148.

Bhargava, P.L.
Problem of Ancient Indian Chronology. 10, 1978-79, pp. 118-122.

Bhatt, S.K.
Archaeological Explorations in Basti District (U.P.). 3, 1969-70, pp. 77-78.

Bhattacharya, D.K., Chakrabarti, Sima and Chakrabarti, Dilip K. ***et al***
Microliths Around Santiniketan. 10, 1978-79, pp. 83-86.

Bhattacharya, P.B.
Indus Valley Civilization—An Aryan Culture? 11, 1979-80, pp. 140-145.

Bhattacharya, S.K.
Buddhist Relic–Caskets in Indian Museums. 17, 1986-87, pp. 43-49.

Bimson
Extract from R.E.M. Wheeler's "Early India and Pakistan". London, 1959, p. 30–5, 1971-72, pp. 61-62.

Bisht, R.S.
Dholavira: A New Horizon of the Indus Civilization. 20, 1989-90, pp. 71-82.

Chakrabarti, Dilip K.
Comments on C.C. Lamberg-Karlovsky's Paper on 'Trade Mechanisms in Indus-Mesopotamian Interrelations'. 7, 1974, pp. 74-75.

Concept of Urban Revolution and the Indian Context. 6, 1972-73, pp. 27-32.

Iron and Urbanization: An Examination of the Indian Context. 15, 1984-85, pp. 68-74.

Pre-Industrial Mines of India. 16, 1985-86, pp. 65-71.

Reserved Slip Ware in the Harappan Context. 8, 1975-76, pp. 158-164.

Some Theoretical Aspects of Early Indian Urban Growth. 7, 1974, pp. 87-89.

Study of the Iron Age in India. 13& 14, 1981-83, pp. 81-85.

— and **Bhattacharya, D.K. and Chattopadhyay, R.K.**
Lithic Industries of Bankura. 11, 1979-80, pp. 39-48.

— and **Chattopadhyay, R.K.**
Parihati, a Mediaeval Smelting Site in Midnapur District, West Bengal. 12, 1980-81, pp. 161-163.

— and **Nag, A.K. and Chakrabarti, D.K.**
Archaeological Reconnaissance in Birbhum. 10, 1978-79, pp. 25-32.

Champaklakshmi, R.
Archaeology and Tamil Literary Tradition. 8, 1975-76, pp. 110-122.

Chattopadhyaya, B.D.
Indian Archaeology and the Epic Traditions. 8, 1975-76, pp. 67-72.

Chaturvedi, Gayatri
Interpretation of Function of Microlithic Tool (Lunate) through Microwear Examination. 22, 1991-92, pp. 5-12.

Chitalwala, Y.M.
Comments on Subsistence Pattern of an Early Farming Community of Western India. 8, 1975-76, p. 140.

Chitkara, Poonam
Depiction of Cattle Motifs on Amri pottery (A Comparative Study with Baluchistan). 9, 1977-78, pp. 92-96.

Conrad, Roswitha
Domestic Animals in the Early Cultures of India. 7, 1974, pp. 76-77.

De, Sudhin and Chattopadhyay, Pranab K.
Archaeometallurgical Studies at Kankrajhor and Dhuliapur. 20, 1989-90, pp. 115-17.

Deo, S.B.
Historical Archaeology: Review and Perspective. 13 & 14, 1981-83, pp. 87-85.

New Evidence of Hinayana Buddhism in Vidarbha. 6, 1972-73, pp. 84-86.

New Painted Pottery from Vidarbha. 1, 1967-68, pp. 36-38.

Deshpande, M.N.
Session on NBP. 5, 1971-72, p. 37.

Session on OCP (Inaugural Speech). 5, 1971-72, pp. 5-7.

Session on OCP. 5, 1971-72, pp. 26-27.

Devasahayam, N.
Unearthed Copper Antennae Sword of Tamil Nadu. 12, 1980-81, p. 129.

Dhavalikar, M.K.
Chalcolithic Burials: The Tekwada Evidence. 2, 1968-69, pp. 35-40.

Chalcolithic Cultures: A Socio–Economic Perspective. 13 & 14, 1981-83, pp. 63-80.

Daimabad—A Rediscovery. 3, 1969-70, pp. 34-43.

Early Warehouse on the Western Coast. 9, 1977-78, pp. 100-103.

New Archaeology and the Indian Situation. 10, 1978-79, pp. 33-38.

Settlement Archaeology of Inamgaon. 8, 1975-76, pp. 44-54.

Some Aspects of the Chalcolithic Cultures of Central India. 4, 1970-71, pp. 24-30.

— and **Jamkhedker, A.P.**
Ksetrapala shrine at Kandhar. 20, 1989-90, pp. 99-106.

— and **Possehl, Gregory L.**
Subsistence Pattern of an Early Farming Community of Western India 7, 1974, pp. 39-46.

Dikshit, K.N.
Bone and Antler Industry from Allahpur, District Meerut. 4, 1970-71, pp. 51-55.

Comments on 'Painted Grey Ware Culture'. 9, 1977-78, pp. 81-83.

Iron Age and Peninsular India. 22, 1991-92, pp. 31-34.

Is the EarlyPottery from Kausambi Harappan? 11, 1979-80, pp. 103-105.

Late Harappan Culture — A Reappraisal. 13 & 14, 1981-83, pp. 51-61.

Legacy of Indus Civilization in North India. 21, 1990-91, pp. 17-20.

Note on the National Museum, Bahrain. 12, 1980-81, pp. 163-164.

Session on NBP. 5, 1971-72, pp. 37-38.

Session on OCP. 5, 1971-72, pp. 8-9.

— and **Sinha, A.K.**
Ganeshwar Culture — An Appraisal. 11, 1979-80, pp. 120-122.

Dogra, S.D.
Greek or Yavana Donors in Ancient India. 8, 1975-76, pp. 185-190.

Pella: Where Alexander the Great was Born. 7, 1974, pp. 106-107.

Francis, Peter
The Areca-nut Object: Is it a Bead?. 10, 1978-79, pp. 95-99.

Frankfort, H.P.
About the Shortughai Sequence from Mature Harappan to Late Bactrian: Bronze Age in Eastern Bacteria (N.E. Afghanistan). 10, 1978-79, pp. 91-94.

Gardin, J.C.
The Development of Eastern Bactria in Pre-Classical Times. 10, 1978-79, pp. 8-13.

Gaur, R.C.
An Appraisal of the Protohistoric Problems of the Ganga-Yamuna Doab. 4, 1970-71, pp. 42-50.

The Aryans—A Fresh Appraisal. 12, 1980-81, pp. 133-135.

Excavations at Daulatpur (District Bulandshahar) and Its Significance. 17, 1986-87, p. 56.

Session on NBP. 5, 1971-72, p. 34.

Seession on OCP. 5, 1971-72, pp. 10-12.

Terracotta Discs. 10, 1978-79, pp. 100-101.

Ghosh, A.
At Random (Presidential Address). 8, 1975-76, pp. 123-125.

Comments on "Concept of Urban Revolution". 6, 1972-73, pp. 34-35.

Megaliths in Yemen Arab Republic. 7, 1974, pp. 81-82.

Session on NBP. 5, 1971-72 p. 38.

Session on OCP. 5, 1971-72, pp. 27-28.

Ghosh, Ashok K. and Chaudhury, Dipankar
On Flake-Blade Element in India. 19, 1988-89, pp. 31-37.

Ghosh, N.C.
Session on NBP. 5, 1971-72, p. 34.

Session on OCP. 5, 1971-72 pp. 13-14.

(A) Stylized Human faced Mask from a Megalithic Burial. 6, 1972-73, pp. 74-75.

— and **Nag, Arun K., Chattopadhyay, Pranab K.**
(The) Archaeological background and Iron Sample from Hatigra. 18, 1987-88, pp. 21-27.

— and **Nag, S.**
Excavations at Hatikara: A Chalcolithic Site in West-Bengal. 15, 1984-85, p. 116.

— and **Sharma, R.P.**
A Note on the Excavation at Virbhadra. 8, 1975-76, pp. 180-181.

Golson, Jack
World Archaeological Congress. 21, 1990-91, pp. 99-101.

Gulliaume, O.
Coins and Small Finds of Indian Origin in Ai-Khanum (Afghanistan). 16, 1985-86, pp. 87-88.

Gupta, Jagdish
(A) Terracotta Medallion from Shahabad, District Hardoi, U.P. 6, 1972-73, pp. 90-91.

Gupta, Kalyan Priya
New Evidence from Kolhua Pillar. 11, 1979-80, pp. 145-147.

Gupta, M.N.
The Authors of the Indus Seal Texts or The Indus Seal Motifs.12, 1980-81, pp. 47-53.

Compoundable Prosodic Signs in the Indus Script. 10, 1978-79, pp. 109-115.

Gupta, Parmeshwari Lal
Numismatics and Archaeology. 18, 1987-88, pp. 85-88.

Gupta, S.P.
(The) Alleged Upper Palaeolithic Bone Mother Goddess from Belan. 11, 1979-80, p. 116.

Copper Hoard Implements in the National Museum Collection: 1985-86. 16, 1985-86, pp. 45-46.

Determining the Techniques of Handmade and Wheel Turned Pottery by Microscopic Analysis. 2, 1968-69, pp. 23-25.

(The) Development of Early Saiva Art: Indian Architecture with Special Reference to Andhra Pradesh. 11, 1979-80, p. 173.

Gulf of Oman: The Original Home of Indian Megaliths. 4, 1970-71, pp. 4-18.

Longer Chronology of the Indus-Saraswati Civilization. 23, 1992-93, pp. 21-29.

(A) Model for Understanding the First Urbanization in India. 6, 1972-73, pp. 42-50.

(A) New Tool-Type of the 'Copper Hoards'. 11, 1979-80, pp. 127-128.

Origin of the Form of Harappan Culture: A New Proposition. 8, 1975-76, pp. 141-146.

(The) Relationship Between the Chalcolithic Culture of India and the Chust Culture of the Farghana Valley, USSR. 1, 1967-68, pp. 47-53.

Session on NBP. 5, 1971-72, pp. 35-36.

Session on OCP. 5, 1971-72, pp. 7-8.

Studies in the Archaeology and Palaeoanthropology of South Asia. 12, 1980-81, pp. 169-172.

Two Urbanizations in India: A Side Study in Their Social-Structure. 7, 1974, pp. 53-60.

Writing Indian Art History: A Search for Valid Approach. 11, 1979-80, pp. 68-73.

— and **Kesarwani , Arun**
Herding as the Backdrop to the Growth of Agriculture in West Asia and South Asia. 12, 1980-81, pp. 101-111.

— and **Pant, P.C., Dikshit, K.N., Pande, B.M.**
Highlights of the International Symposium on Radiocarbon and Indian Archaeology-1972. 6, 1972-73, pp. 80-83.

Gurumurthi, A.
Jain Vestiges at Renukonda Fort. 22, 1991-92, pp. 103-107.

Mahāmrityunjaya in art. 18, 1987-88, pp. 102-105.

Hasan, S. Jamal
The Distribution and Types of Beads in the Gangetic Valley. 11, 1979-80, pp. 131-140.

Some Indeterminate Terracotta Objects—A Study. 10, 1978-79, pp. 104-105.

Hashmi, Syed Anis
Ethno-Archaeology of the Traditional Ceremonial Pottery of Gujarat. 19, 1988-89, pp. 60-63.

Hegde, K.T.M.
Ancient Indian Pottery-Kilns. 9, 1977-78, pp. 109-111.

Extract from "Current Science" December 20, 1966, 35, No. 24, p. 623. 5, 1971-72, p. 62.

Extracts from 'Physics and Chemistry in Indian Archaeology', Paper Read at the Annual Conference, Indian Archaeological Society, Nagpur, 1970. 5, 1971-72, pp. 63-64.

Laboratory Studies in the Jokha Midden Soil Samples. 3, 1969-70, pp. 9-14.

Use of Caliche as a Chronological and Environmental Tool in the Study of Late Quaternary Formations in Gujarat and Rajasthan. 8, 1975-76, pp. 37-43.

Irwin, John
(The) Heliodorus Pillar at Besnagar. 8, 1975-76, pp: 166-176.

Jayaswal, Vidula
(A) Note on the Influence of Raw Material on Blank-detaching Techniques. 6, 1972-73, pp. 64-70.

(A) Techno–typological Review of the Middle Palaeolithic Cultures of India. 7, 1974, pp. 13-16.

Jha, Achyutanand
Identification of Pundravardhana. 21, 1990-91, pp. 81-84.

Joshi, Jagat Pati
Harappan Culture: Emergence of a New Picture. 13 & 14, 1981-83, pp. 51-54.

(A) Note on the Excavation at Bhagwanpura. 8, 1975-76, pp. 178-180.

Surkotada: A Chronological Assessment. 7, 1974, pp. 34-38.

Joshi, M.C.
Archaeology and Indian Tradition–Some Observations. 8, 1975-76, pp. 98-102.

Ayodhya: Mythical and Real. 11, 1979-80, pp. 107-109.

Comments on "Concept of Urban Revolution". 6, 1972-73, p. 36 B.

Composite Images of Lakshmi and Vishnu: Some Observations. 11, 1979-80, pp. 81-83.

Early Historical Urban Growth in India: Some observations. 7, 1974, pp. 90-91.

Early Representation of Buddha and Buddhist Traditions in *Aśokāvadāna*. 21, 1990-91, pp. 1-6.

Sabz-Burj: An Early Mughal Tomb. 6, 1972-73, pp. 87-89.

Session on NBP. 5, 1971-72, pp. 36.

Session on OCP. 5, 1971-72, p. 13.

(A) Terracotta Medallion from Shahabad, District Hardoi, U.P. 6, 1972-73, p.91.

— and **Sinha, A.K.**
Chronology of Mathura—An Assessment. 10, 1978-79, pp. 39-44.

Joshi, Maheshwar, P.
Dots, Cup-marks and Pits vis-a-vis the Megaliths–New Evidences from Kumaon. 16, 1985-86, pp. 25-28.

Joshi, R.V.
Archaeological Chemistry in India—Some Aspects. 13 & 14, 1981-83, pp. 111-114.

— and **Deotare, B.C., Kshirsagar, A.A.**
Chemistry of Deccan Chalcolithic Deposits from Daimabad and Inamgaon. 10, 1978-79, pp. 80-81.

— and **Marathe, A.R.**
Metrical Analysis of Handaxes from Chirki-on-Pravara (Western Maharashtra, India). 8, 1975-76, pp. 3-12.

Joshi, S.K.
Human Settlements in Goa till 16th Century: An overview. 23, 1992-93 pp. 64-66.

Kajale, M.D. and Deotare, B.C.
Pollen Analysis and Chemical Examinations of a Prehistoric Lake Site at Damdama. 19, 1988-89, pp. 27-30.

Kala, Jayantika
Rare Object from Kosam. 15, 1984-85, p. 120.

Kennedy, Kenneth A.R., Burrow, Christopher B. and Loveu, Nancy C.
Mesolithic Human Remains from the Gangetic Plain Sarai Nahar Rai. 15, 1984-85, pp. 1-55.

Khan, E.
Mammalian Fossil Fauna: a Most Modern Tool for Dating the Pleistocene Deposits. 4, 1970-71, pp. 31-41.

Khan, Mohd. Abdul Waheed
Armenian Cemetery of Hyderabad. 6, 1972-73, p. 79.

Khan, Mohd. Afral
Urban and Palace Waterworks During the Mughal Period. 19, 1988-89, pp. 46-49.

Khanna, A.N.
Black Lustrous Ware of Himachal Pradesh. 10, 1978-79, pp. 117-118.

Khare, M.D.
Comments on 'Heliodorus Pillar' at Besnagar. 8, 1975-76, pp. 176-178.

Dangwada (Ujjain) —A Chalcolithic Site. 11, 1979-80, pp. 117-120.

Neo-Chalcolithic Remains at Rangai (Vidisha). 12, 1980-81, pp. 55-57.

Khatri, A.P.
Handaxe and Chopper–Chopping Tool Tradition: The Ideas of Two Culture Theory of Early Palaeolithic in Asia. 9, 1977-78, pp. 3-14.

Khazanchi, T.N. and Dikshit, K.N.
Grey Ware Culture of Northern Pakistan, Jammu & Kashmir and Punjab. 9, 1977-78, pp. 47-51.

Krishna Deva
Comments on 'Concept of Urban Revolution'. 6, 1972-73, pp. 33-34.

Session on OCP. 5, 1971-72, pp. 15-16.

Krishna Kumar
Study in the Stone Age of Khajuraho in Central India. 3, 1969-70, pp. 89-104.

Krishna Kumari, M.
Kāmeśvara Temple at Galiavalli. 16, 1985-86, pp. 55-58.

Krishna Murthy, K.
Domestic Art Delineated in the Gandhara Reliefs. 7, 1974, pp. 96-103.

Note on the Stucco Figure of Jambhala from Amaravati in Andhra Pradesh. 6, 1972-73, pp. 76-78.

Kumar, Vijaya
Discovery of Ochre Coloured Pottery from Noh, District Bharatpur. 5, 1971-72, pp. 43-44.

Lal, B.B.
Archaeology in India Since Independence: Some Random Thoughts. 12, 1980-81, pp. 15-21.

Are the Defences of Kausambi Really as Old as 1025 B.C.? 11, 1979-80, pp. 88-95.

Ayodhya of the Valmiki Ramayana: An Energizing Debate on Its Identification. 16, 1985-86, pp. 79-86.

Banganga-Beas Palaeolithic Industry: A Look Back. 11, 1979-80, pp. 1-10.

Chronology of Painted Grey Ware. Did the Painted Grey Ware Continue up to the Mauryan Times? 9, 1977-78, pp. 64-80.

Extract from "Indian Archaeology- A Review" 1955-56, pp. 56-57. 5, 1971-72, p. 61.

Further Note on the Direction of Writing in the Harappan Script. 1, 1967-68, pp. 15-16.

A Note on the Excavation at Saipai. 5, 1971-72, pp. 46-49.

Ochre Coloured Pottery—A Geochronological Study. 5, 1971-72, pp. 49-58.

Perhaps the Earliest Ploughed Field so far Excavated Anywhere in the World. 4, 1970-71, pp. 1-3.

Problems of Indian Archaeology: Planning Ahead. 8, 1975-76, pp. 126-131.

So-called Śyenachiti at Kausambi: A Fallen Brick Mass. 15, 1984-85, pp. 86-98.

Some Aspects of the Archaeological Evidence Relating to the Indus Script. 7, 1974, pp. 20-24.

Was Ayodhya a Mythical City? 10, 1978-79, pp. 45-49.

When did Udayana rule? In the Sixth Century B.C. or the Sixteenth Century A.D.? An Assessment of the Dating of the Palace–Complex at Kausambi. 15, 1984-85, pp. 80-85.

— and **Dikshit, K.N.**
Pariar—An Eastern Outpost of the Painted Grey Ware. 11, 1979-80, pp. 26-31.

Sringaverapura: A key site for the Protohistory and Early History of the Central Ganga Valley. 10, 1978-79, pp. 1-7.

— and **Sharma, K.K.**
Date of King Dhanadeva of Kosala: A Re–examination of the Palaeographic and Historical Evidence. 19, 1988-89, pp. 38-42.

Lal, Makkhan
Copper Hoard Culture of India: A Reassessment. 12, 1980-81, pp. 65-77.

Iron at Ahar: A comment. 18, 1987-88, pp. 109-112.

Population, Distribution and Its Movement During the Second and First Millennia B.C. in the Indo–Gangetic Divide and Upper Ganga Plain. 18, 1987-88, pp. 35-53.

— and **Salahuddin**
Deogarh Acheulian Assemblage: A Preliminary Report. 20, 1989-90, pp. 64-70.

Lamberg-Karlovsky, C.C.
Trade Mechanisms in Indus–Mespotamian Interrelations. (Published in the Journal of the American Oriental Society, Vol. 92, No. 2, 1972) (Readings in Indian Archaeology) 6, 1972-73, pp. 103-117.

Leakey, Richard
Two and half Million Year Old Human Skull Found. 6, 1972-73, p. 113.

Madhu Bala
Maltese Cross on Protohistoric Pottery. 11, 1979-80, pp. 129-131.

Madhukar, Mahesh Prasad
Bronze Age Culture of Thailand. 16, 1985-86, pp. 59-62.

Mahadevan, Iravatham
Cult Object on Unicorn Seals: A Sacred Filter ? 13 & 14, 1981-83, pp. 165-186.

Indus Sealing from Hulas. 11, 1979-80, p. 117.

Recent Advances in the Study of the Indus Script. 9, 1977-78, pp. 34-42.

Mahalingam, T.V.
University of Madras (Archaeology in Universities Series). 2, 1968-69, pp. 61-62.

Malaiya, Sudha
Notes on Sculptures in the Early Art of Central India. 16, 1985-86, pp. 47-54.

Malik, D.K.
Slip on Pottery —A Case Study. 11, 1979-80, pp. 164-165.

Malik, S.C.
Role of Theory in the Study of Archaeology in India. 6, 1972-73, pp. 1-11.

Malla, Bansilal
Sculptural Art in Payar Temple. 18, 1987-88, pp. 106-108.

Mani, B.R.
Excavations at Lalkot 1991-92, and Further Explorations in Delhi. 22, 1991-92, pp. 75-87.

Identification of Setavya, the Ancient City of Kosala with Siswania and Its Terracotta Art. 21, 1990-91, pp. 43-49.

Margabandhu, C.
Note on Some Ancient Indian Mirrors. 7, 1974, pp. 94-95.

— and **Gaur, G.S.**
Sanghol Excavations 1987: Some New Evidence. 17, 1986-87, pp. 1-4.

Some Fresh Evidence from Sanghol Excavations 1986. 16, 1985-86, pp. 73-78.

— and **Sharma, R.P.**
Exploration Along the Sahibi River in District Gurgaon. 10, 1978-79, pp. 14-19.

Mate, Madhukar, Shripad
Early Historic Fortifications in the Ganga Valley. 3, 1969-70, pp. 58-69.

Meena, B.R.
Recent Exploration in the Valley of Khari and Mansi Rivers, Rajasthan: With Special Reference to the Chalcolithic Sites. 16, 1985-86, pp. 17-23.

Mehendale, M.A.
Prof. Thieme's Etymology of Skt. 'asi' and Its Bearing on the Iron-Age in India. 10, 1978-79, pp. 79-80.

Mehta, R.N.
Economic Pattern of India During the Early Iron Age (1000 B.C.-100 A.D.) Gujarat. 9, 1977-78, pp. 52-55.

Mediaeval Archaeology. 13 & 14, 1981-83, pp. 97-102.

Two Earth-Works from Gujarat. 3, 1969-70, pp. 54-57.

— and **Jamindar, Rasesh**
Salvage Archaeology: Ahmadabad, 1984. 15, 1984-85, pp. 111-115.

Mishra, Suresh Chandra
Archaeological Testimony of Surunga and the Mauryanism of the Arthasastra of Kautilya. 19, 1988-89, pp. 74-76.

Misra, V.N.
Acheulian Industry of Rock Shelter III F-23 at Bhimbetka, Central India: A Preliminary Study. 8, 1975-76, pp. 13-36.

Archaeological and Ethnographic Evidence for the Hafting and Use of Microliths and Related Tools. 7, 1974, pp. 3-12.

— and **Rajaguru, S.N., Wasson, R.J., Singh, G. and Agrawal, D.P.**
Further Light on Lower Palaeolithic Occupation and Palaeoenvironment in Semiarid Zone of Rajasthan. 11, 1979-80, pp. 11-18.

Mitra, D.
Recent Archaeological Activities in India. 12, 1980-81, pp. 1-7.

Mitra, S.K.
Discovery of an Early Inscription from Pitalkhora. 21, 1990-91, pp. 84-85.

Unique Art Relief from Ajanta. 22, 1991-92, pp. 133-136.

Mittal, R.S.
Session on OCP. 5, 1971-72, pp. 25-26.

Mittre, Vishnu
Inter-relations Between Archaeology and Plant Sciences. 1, 1967-68, pp. 4-14.

Status of Barley in Indian Archaeobotany with Remarks on the Aryan Hypothesis. 3, 1969-70, pp. 1-2.

— and **Gupta, H.P.**
Plant Remains from Ancient Bhatkuli, District Amraoti, Maharashtra. 2, 1968-69, pp. 21-22.

— and **Savithri, R.**
Ancient Plant Economy at Inamgaon. 8, 1975-76, pp. 55-62.

Ancient Plant Economy at Noh, Rajasthan. 7, 1974, pp. 77-80.

— and **Sharma, Chhaya, Saxena, A.K., Prasad, Kamla, Bhattacharya, A. and Chauhan, M.S.**
Pollen Stratigraphy of India. 13 & 14, 1981-83, pp. 115-122.

Moghrdam, Parveen and Chakrabarti, Dilip K.

Channel-spouted Vessel from Hissar. 8, 1975-76, pp. 164-165.

Mohammad, K.K.
Glazed Ware in India. 15, 1984-85, pp. 105-110.

Some Literary References to Chinese Pottery in India. 11, 1979-80, pp. 78-80.

Mohan, Vijneshu
Role of the Individual's Perception and Important Explanatory Modees in Archaeology. 21, 1990-91, pp. 51-56.

An Optimal Modelling Exercise for the Harappan Civilization with special Reference to its Regional context in Haryana, India. 23, 1992-93, pp. 13-20.

Mohanty, Pradeep
Stone Age Research in Keonjhar District, Orissa. 17, 1986-87, pp. 54-55.

Mohapatra, G.C.
Lower Palaeolithic in India. 13 & 14, 1981-83, pp. 1-8.

Neolithic of Western Sub-Himalaya. 10, 1978-79, pp. 20-24.

— and **Saroj, Hari Mohan**
Discovery of Lithic Artifacts in Jammu Area. 2, 1968-69, pp. 11-12.

Momin, K.N.
Excavation at Zekhada. 12, 1980-81, pp. 120-125.

Moorti, Udairavi S.
Socio-economic Aspects of Megalithic Vidarbha. 15, 1984-85, pp. 56-67.

Evidence of Social Differentiation and Socio-political Organization during the Megalithic Period in south India. 20, 1989-90, pp. 1-64.

Mouli, N. Chandra
(An) Attempt towards the Interpretation of Rock Paintings at Kethavaram, Kurnool District, Andhra Pradesh. 18, 1987-88, pp. 72-78.

Mughal, Rafique
Early Harappa Culture Phase: A Reply. 9, 1977-78, pp. 84-87.

Mukherjee, B.N.
Note an 'Archaeology of Early Mediaeval Towns in Bengal'. 15, 1984-85, pp. 121-122.

Mullick, C.C.
Indian Indonesia. 17, 1986-87, pp. 33-37.

Murty, M.L.K.
Symbiosis and Traditional Behaviour in the Subsistence Economics of the Kunchapuri Yerukulas of south India: A Predictive Model. 10, 1978-79, pp. 50-61.

Upper Palaeolithic Culture in India. 13 & 14, 1981-83, pp. 15-25.

Nag, A.K. and Chakrabarti, Dilip K.
"Copper Hoards" from West Bengal. 9, 1977-78, pp. 97-99.

Nagarch, B.L. and Trivedi, P.K.
Note on Aguncha, District Bilwara, Rajasthan. 10, 1978-79, p. 106.

Nagaswamy, R.
Restrictions on Arresting Person: An Ancient Example. 17, 1986-87, pp. 31-32.

Narasimhaiah, B.
Restoration of Angkor Vat (Cambodia): Indian Crusade. 22, 1991-92, pp. 109-113.

Nath, Amarendra
Arambha; A Vākāṭaka Site in Vidarbha. 22, 1991-92, pp. 69-74.

Archaeology of the Wardha Wainganga Divide. 20, 1989-90, pp. 93-98.

Nath, J.
Sambara or Trailokyavijaya: Fresh Identification. 17, 1986-87, pp. 57-58.

Siddhaikavira Image from Nalanda. 17, 1986-87, pp. 58-59.

Nauriyal, K.C.
Northern Black Polished and Other Associated Wares from Ropar. 21, 1990-91, pp. 87-89.

Nautiyal, K.P. and Khanduri, B.M.
Excavations at Moradhwaj–A Note. 10, 1978-79, pp. 86-87.

Excavations of a Vedic Brick Altar at Purola, District Uttarkashi, Central Himalaya. 19, 1988-89, pp. 68-69.

Nautiyal, K.P., Khanduri, B.M., Nautiyal, Vinod., Rajput, D. L. and Bhatt, R.K.
Painted Grey Ware Culture in Garhwal Himalaya: New Evidence and Interpretation. 17, 1986-87, pp. 11-14.

Nautiyal, K.P., Khanduri, B.M., Nautiyal, Vinod., Rajpur, D.L.
Thapli: A Painted Grey Ware Site in Garhwal. 10, 1978-79, pp. 94-95.

Nautiyal, Vinod, Nautiyal, K.P., Khanduri, B.M. Rajput, D.L., *et al*
Beginning of Iron Age in Garhwal, Mid-Central Himalaya: An Ecological Overview. 21, 1990-91, pp. 29-35.

Negi, Baldev Singh
Distribution of Painted Grey Ware Sites in District Bharatpur (Rajasthan). 12, 1980-81, pp. 129-132.

Neumayer, Erwin
Music and Musical Instrument in Indian Rock-Art. 23, 1992-93, pp. 69-84.

On the Identification of Bhakti-Deities in Rock Pictures. 23, 1992-93, pp. 53-60.

Rock Pictures in Orissa. 22, 1991-92, pp. 13-24.

Explorations Along the Banganga River, District Bharatpur, Rajasthan. 17, 1986-87, pp. 5-10.

Nigam, J.S.
Session on OCP. 5, 1971-72, p.12.

Ota, S.B.
Khaparkhera: A Submergible Chalcolithic Site. 21, 1990-91, pp. 76-77.

Paddayya, K.
Prehistoric Research in India: As Viewed by Two Senior American Archaeologists. 19, 1988-89, pp. 77-79.

Padhy, K.P.
Role of Temples in Medieval Orissa. 21, 1990-91, pp. 85-86.

Pal, J.N.
Microlithic Industry of Damdama, Pratapgarh, U.P.: A Preliminary Analysis. 16, 1985-86, pp. 1-5.

Upper Palaeolithic Cultures of the Mid-Son Valley. 12, 1980-81, pp. 23-30.

Pande, Anupa
Art and Its Decorative Outlook. 22, 1991-92, pp. 132-133.

Note on Pindibandha an Ancient Dance Form. 18, 1987-88, pp. 89-92.

Pande, B.M.
Archaeology of Thanesar: A Brief Report on Excavation at Harsh-Ka-Tila. 19, 1988-89, pp. 1-5.

Inscribed Copper Tablets from Mohenjodaro: Some Observations. 21, 1990-91, pp. 25-28.

Inscribed Harappan Material from Kalibangan: Some Remarks on Methodology and Approach. 8, 1975-76, pp. 156-157.

Inscribed Harappan potsherds from Chandigarh. 6, 1972-73, pp. 52-55.

On the Origin of the Harappan Sign. 7, 1974, pp. 25-33.

— and, **Vyas, Narayan**
Early Temple in Gujarat—Excavations at Goraj (Mohadepura). 20, 1989-90, pp. 107-110.

Pande, Hemchandra
On the Decipherment of the Indus Script by Soviet Scholars. 21, 1990-91, pp. 71-72.

Pandey, Deenabandhu
Some Ancient Sketches in Kajuraho Temples. 2, 1968-69 p. 59.

Tribal deity of the Vishaṇins. 1, 1967-68, p. 99.

Pandey, J.N.
Lalapur: An Acheulian Site in District Banda (U.P.). 11, 1979-80, pp. 113-116.

Pandey, R.P.
Significance of Animal fossils in the prehistoric studies of the upper Mahanadi Valley, Central India. 12, 1980-81, pp. 37-46.

Pandya, Suman
Recent Advances in Protohistoric Gujarat. 12, 1980-81, pp. 59-63.

Pant, P.C.
Prehistoric Uttar Pradesh: A rejoinder to the review. 12, 1980-81, pp. 167-169.

Typology in Prehistory. 1, 1967-68, pp. 61-67.

— and **Jayaswal, Vidula**
A Typological Variant within the Middle Palaeolithic Culture Complex of India. 9, 1977-78, pp. 15-33.

Pappu, R.S.
Explorations of Prehistoric Sites in District Bijapur. 4, 1970-71, pp. 58-62.

Parpola, Asko
Bibliographical Aids for the Study of the Indus Civilization: A Critical Survey. 8, 1975-76, pp. 150-156.

Pathak, Anamika
Casing Slab from Nagarjunkonda – A Reappraisal. 19, 1988-89, pp. 72-73.

Pathak, Haldhar
Three Saucer type coins from Varanasi. 16, 1985-86, pp. 89-90.

Pathak, P.V.
Indus Culture Seal of Three Forms and Seven Figures as Pictorial Representation of AV Hymn IV. 37-22, 1991-92, pp. 59-63.

Lady of the Beasts or the Lord of the Beasts. A Reappraisal. 21, 1990-91, pp. 57-64.

Patnaik, J.K., and Tripathy, B.K.
Ships and Shipping in Orissan Art. 23, 1992-93, pp. 61-63.

Possehl, Gregory L.
Culture and Process. 9, 1977-78, pp. 43-46.

Harappans in Saurashtra: New Chronological Considerations. 22, 1991-92, pp 25-29.

Indian Archaeology — A Review: Guide to Excavated Sites. 1953-54 through 1984-85. 18, 1987-88, pp. 113-171.

— and **Chitwala, Y.M., Rissman, Paul and Wagner, Gail.**
Excavations at Rojdi: 1982-83. 13 & 14, 1981-83, pp. 155-163.

Prakash, B.
Archaeometallurgical Study of Iron Pillar at Dhar. 20, 1989-90, pp. 118-122.

Prakash, P. Vijaya
Prehistoric Investigation in the Gambheeram Valley: Visakhapatnam Coast. 11, 1979-80, pp. 109-113.

Prasad, Ajit Kumar
Excavation at Taradih. 12, 1980-81, pp. 138-139.

Prasad, Pushpa
Credit and Mortgage Documents in the Lekhapaddhati. 18, 1987-88, pp. 93-101.

Rai, S. and Roy, T.N.
Mossbuaer studies of Black Slipped and Northern Black Polished wares. 12, 1980-81, pp. 165-167.

Rajaguru, S.N.
Some New Fossil discoveries from western Maharashtra, India. 2, 1968-69, pp. 16-20.

Rajan, K.
Iron and Gemstone Industries as Revealed from Kodumanal Excavations. 20, 1989-90, pp. 111-112.

Megalithic Culture in North Arcot Region. 22, 1991-92, pp. 35-46.

Ramachandran, K.S.
Cairn Burials of Baluchistan, Makran and South-East Iran: Their Character and Chronology. 7, 1974, pp. 82-87.

Chronology of the Indian Megaliths–Some Considerations. 3, 1969-70, pp. 107-109.

Gulf of Oman: Original Home of the Indian Megaliths– A Reappraisal. 6, 1972-73, pp. 20-26

Rana, R.S.
New Light on Jhusi Culture in Allahabad, U.P. 17, 1986-87, p.60.

Rao, S.N.
Regional Variations in the Indian Middle Stone Age Culture with Special Reference to Nalgonda in Andhra Pradesh. 2, 1968-69, pp.13-15.

Rao, V.V.
Ornithology in Protohistoric Archaeology of India. 6, 1972-73, pp. 56-59.

Rawson, P.S.
Extracts from 'The Surface Treatment of Early Indian Pottery', "Man" 1953, Art. 58. pp. 41-42–5, 1971-72, pp. 59-60.

Ray, Nihar Ranjan
Technology and Social Change in Early Indian History: A Note Posing a Theoretical Question. 8, 1975-76, pp. 132-138.

Roux, Valentine
Ethnoarchaeological Survey on Ceramic Production. 16, 1985-86, pp. 63-64.

— and **Pelegrin, Cacques**
Knapping Technique and Craft Specialization: An Ethnoarchaeological Investigation in Gujarat. 19, 1988-89, pp. 50-59.

Roy, S.B.
Harappan Chronology: An Integrated Study. 7, 1974, pp. 65-69.

Notes on Cross–Contacts of Vedic India with West Asia and Iran. 8, 1975-76, pp. 146-150.

Roy, Sita Ram
Urbanisation of Vaiśāli. 12, 1980-81, pp136-138.

Roy, T.N.
Excavations at Manjhi. 1983-85: A Preliminary Report. 16, 1985-86,pp. 29-32.

Note on Makara Figurines. 3, 1969-70, pp. 105-106.

Suggested Classification of Northern Black Polished Ware. 10, 1978-79, pp. 106-109.

Saar, S.S.
Drawing in Archaeology: Suggestions. 10, 1978-79, pp. 115-117.

Use of Orthographic Projection in Archaeological Drawing. 12, 1980-81, pp. 159-161.

Sahi, M.D.N.
Stratigraphical Position of the N.B.P. Ware in the Upper Ganga Basin and its Date. 7, 1974, pp. 91-94.

Salahuddin
Biostratigraphy of the Central Narmada Valley with Special Reference to Hexaprotodon Spp. 18, 1987-88, pp. 1-20

— and **Makkhan Lal**
Deogarh Acheulian Assemblage: A Preliminary Report. 20, 1989-90, pp. 65-70.

Sali, S.A.
Unique Terracotta Figurine from the Jorwe Levels of Daimabad. 11, 1979-80, pp. 128-129.

Sankalia, H.D.
Archaeology and the Ramayana or Dating the Ramayana. 1, 1967-68, pp. 1-3.

Cemetery 'H' Culture. 6. 1972-73, pp. 12-19.

Deccan College Post–Graduate and Research Institute (Archaeology in Universities series). 2, 1968-69, p.60.

Functional significance of the O.C.P. and P.G.W. shapes and Associated objects. 7, 1974, pp. 47-52.

Prehistoric Colonization in India: Archaeological and Literary Evidence. 8, 1975-76, pp. 72-86.

Saran, S.C.
Exploration Reveals a Fresh Light on the History of Kisan Bilas, District Kota, Rajasthan. 12, 1980-81, pp. 148-150.

Sarana, Gopala
Sociological framework for Archaeological Research. 8, 1975-76, pp. 183-184.

Saraswat, K.S.
Plant Economy in Ancient Sringaverapura Phase I (c.1050-1000 B.C.).12, 1980-81, pp. 79-80.

Saraswat, K.S.
Plant Economyof Late Harappans at Hulas. 23, 1992-93, pp. 1-12.

Sarkar, H.
On the Conquest of Meluhha by Rimus (2315-2307 B.C.) a Hypothesis. 8, 1975-76, pp. 157-158.

Some Aspects of Megalithic Culture of India. 11, 1979-80, pp. 49-55.

— and **Pande, B.M.**
Note on a Knot Design from Mohenjodaro and its Occurrence in Later Times. 3, 1969-70, pp. 44-48.

Sarma, I.K.
Ceramics and Maritime Routes of India: New Evidence. 21, 1990-91, pp. 37-42.

New Light on Vengipura: Excavations at the Ancient Historical City of Andhradesa. 17, 1986-87, pp. 15-21.

Patapadu Revisited: A New Painted Pottery Culture of South-East India. 1, 1967-68, pp. 68-84.

Sengupta, Aparna
Study of Place-Names and Protophsitoric Cultures in Andhra-Karnataka. 11, 1979-80, pp. 56-58.

Role of Computer in Archaeology. 21, 1990-91, pp. 7-16.

Sengupta, R.
Stuccos in Central Asia and India: A Reappraisal. 12, 1980-81, pp. 91-95.

Timurid Mosque at Balkh in Afghanistan and Development of Mughal Domes in India. 9, 1977-78, pp. 57-63.

Qutb Minar: Strengthening the Foundations. 10, 1978-79, pp. 70-75.

Seshadri, M.
Excavations of an Apsidal Brick Temple at Banavasi, District North Canara. 4, 1970-71, pp. 56-57.

Neolithic Burial from T. Narasipur. 2, 1968-69, pp. 55-56.

Shankara Nath
Pre-Harappan Pottery from District Saharanpur (U.P.). 11, 1979-80, p. 122.

Session on OCP. 5, 1971-72, pp. 14-15.

Sharma, A.K.
Animal Bones from Gufkral–Evidence of Human and Non-Human activities. 12, 1980-81, pp. 31-36.

Evidence of Horse from the Harappan Settlement at Surkotada. 7, 1974, pp. 75-76.

Excavations at Gufkral, 1981. 11, 1979-80, pp. 19-25.

Excavations at Karkabhaat. 21, 1990-91, pp. 21-24.

Excavations at Ladyura, Almora, U.P. 21, 1990-91 pp. 77-79.

Excavations at Vadagokugiri (Meghalaya). 22, 1991-92, pp. 89-96.

Exposing and Conserving a World Heritage Monument. 19, 1988-89, pp. 64-67.

Locating the Graves at Kalibangan. 9, 1977-78, pp. 89-91.

Prehistoric Explorations in Sikkim.10, 1978-79, pp. 82-83.

Sharma, A.K.
The Harappan Horse was buried under the dunes of.... 23, 1992-93, pp. 30-34.

— and **Ota, S.B.**
Anangpur: A Paleolithic Site near Delhi. 21, 1990-91, pp. 73-74.

Sharma, D.P.
Copper Hoard Implements in the National Museum, New Delhi, 1987 Collection. 17, 1986-87, pp. 38-42.

Some New Finds in Fatehpur District., Uttar Pradesh. 11, 1979-80, pp. 655-67.

Sharma, D.V.
Harappan Furnaces. 11, 1979-80, pp. 125-127.

Sharma, G.B. and Kumar, Manmohan
Excavation at Rohira. 12, 1980-81, pp. 125-127.

Sharma, G.R.
Excavations at Baharia, District Shahjahanpur. 5, 1971-72, pp. 42-43.

Sharma R.A.
Agricultural Remains from Madhya Pradesh (India) from

Chalcolithic Period to Mauryan Period. 22, 1991-92, pp. 53-58.

Sharma, R.C.
Development of Sculptural Stone and Terracotta Art in India from the Beginning to the Mauryan Age. 22, 1991-92, pp. 65-68.

Sharma, R.P.
Khatoli—A Protohistoric site in Haryana. 11, 1979-80, pp. 123-1125.

Socio-economic Note on Tribes and Peasants. 6, 1972-73, pp. 60-63.

Sharma, R.S.
Later Vedic Phase and the Painted Grey Ware Culture. 8, 1975-76, pp. 63-67.

Sharma, T.C.
Recent Archaeological Discoveries in North-Eastern India. 7, 1974, pp. 17-19.

Sharma, V.C.
Burnt Brick Structure at Hulas. 11, 1979-80, pp. 148-149.

Defence System in Ancient India based on Literary and Archaeological Evidence. 21, 1990-91, pp. 65-69.

Sharma, Y.D.
Pre-Harappans in Punjab. 11, 1979-80,, pp. 32-38.

Salvage of Archaeological evidence from Bahadrabad. 5, 1971-72, pp. 39-42.

Session on NBP. 5, 1971-72, p.33.

Shastri, Ajay Mitra
Ayodhyā and God Rama. 23, 1992-93, pp. 35-39.

Session on OCP. 5, 1971-72, pp. 21-24.

Shendge, Malati
Harappan and Rigvedic Inter-relations. 8, 1975-76, pp. 103-110.

Shinde, Vasant
Land use Pattern during Chalcolithic Period in the Tapi Basin. 18, 1987-88, pp. 54-60.

Harappan Horned Deity: the Evidence from Padri in Western India. 21, 1990-91, pp. 79-81.

Settlement Archaeology of Kaothe: A Chalcolithic Site in the Tapi Basin. 22, 1991-92, pp. 47-52.

Shukla, B.C.
Archaeological findings from Durvasa. 16, 1985-86, pp. 33-35.

New Gupta Inscription from Kausambi. 16, 1985-86, pp. 85-86.

Siddiqui, W.H.
Prehistory of Dadra and Nagar Haveli. 10, 1978-79, pp. 87-89.

On Tughluq Architecture of Gujarat. 11, 1979-80, pp. 155-158.

Singh, A.K.
Kamquali Copper-plate Inscription of Govindachandra (Vikram year 1197). 22, 1991-92, pp. 117-120.

Kashmir—Where the roots of Western Tibetan Art lie. 12, 1980-81, pp. 145-148.

Singh, A.K., Singh, Ravindra N. & Chaturvedi, Majula
Unique Inscribed Metal Sculpture of Padmapani from Western Himalayas. 22, 1991-92, pp. 136-139.

Singh, Bhagwan
Identification of Soma. 12, 1980-81, pp. 154-157.

Singh, Bhupendra Pal
Microlithic Site from Shahabad (Bihar). 1, 1967-68, pp. 100-103.

Middle Stone Age Site on River Durgawati in District Shahabad, Bihar. 3, 1969-70, pp. 70-73.

Singh, Birendra Pratap
Early Farming Communities of Kaimur Foot Hills. 19, 1988-89, pp. 6-18.

Chalcolithic Culture of Southern Bihar as revealed by the Exploration and Excavation in District Rohtas. 20, 1989-90, pp. 83-92.

Khairadih—a Chalcolithic Settlement. 18, 1987-88, pp. 28-34.

Singh, Gurdip
Abstract from "The Indus Valley Culture" (Readings in Indian Archaeology Series). 4, 1970-71, pp. 68-76.

Singh, M.
Analytical Investigation of Indian Bronzes. 21, 1990-91, pp. 96-97.

Singh, M. Jitendra
Prehistoric Archaeological Studies in Manipur. 12, 1980-81, pp. 114-115.

Singh, Purushottam
Burial Practices in the Neolithic cultures of south India. 1, 1967-68,, pp. 31-35.

Megalithic Remains in the Aravallis. 2, 1968-69, pp. 46-48.

— and **Lal Makkhan Singh, Ashok Kumar**
Excavations at Narhan 1983-85. 15, 1984-85, pp. 117-120.

— Singh, Ashok Kumar and Singh, Indrajeet
Excavations at Imlidih Khurd. 22, 1991-92, pp. 120-122.

Singh, Ravindra, N.
Antiquity of Gold-Glasses in India. 12, 1980-81, pp. 157-159.

—and **Abdurajakov, A.A.**
Report on the Chemical Analysis of the Glasses from Khairadih. 21, 1990-91, pp. 92-96.

Singh, R.N. and Jain, K.K.
Studies in Ancient Building Materials: A Note on Bhitari Plaster. 10, 1978-79. pp. 103-104.

Singh, S.P.
Rigvedic Base of the Paśupati Seal of Mohenjodaro. 19, 1988-89, pp. 19-26.

Singh, Y.B.
Archaeology and the Problem of Regional Identity. 12, 1980-81, pp. 150-151.

Indus Civilization, Echoes in Later Literature. 16, 1985-86, pp. 15-16.

Sinha, A.K.
Historical Urbanization —A Suggestive Date. 11, 1979-80, pp. 151-155.

Ivory and Bone Plaquettes—A Note. 10, 1978-79, pp. 101-103.

Rock Engravings at Tabo, Distt. Lahul and Spiti, Himachal Pradesh. 21, 1990-91, pp. 90-92.

Sinha, B.K.
Excavations at Golbai Sasan, District Puri, Orissa. 21, 1990-91, pp. 74-76.

Excavations at Golbai Sasan, Dist. Puri, Orissa. 23, 1992-93, pp. 48-50.

Sinha, B.P.
Indian Tradition and Archaeology. 13 & 14, 1981-83, pp. 103-109.

Crystal Human figure from Sonepur. 2, 1968-69, pp. 51-52.

Some Rare Antiquities from Recent Excavations in Bihar. 6, 1972-73, pp. 71-73.

Sinha, K.K.
Session on NBP. 5, 1971-72, pp. 29-33, p. 38.

Session on OCP. 5, 1971-72, pp. 24-25.

Use of the Terms 'Prehistory' and 'Protohistory' in Indian Archaeology. 1, 1967-68, pp. 39-41.

Sonawane, V.H.
Rotary Quern Mining Industry at Kakachia, District Panch Mahals, Gujarat. 11, 1979-80, pp. 149-150.

Stupas: A Rare Depiction in Rock Paintings of Gujarat, India. 23, 1992-93, pp. 66-69.

Soundara Rajan, K.V.
Changing Face of Archaeological Studies. 1, 1967-68, pp. 24-30.

Eco-Functional Frame of Early Man — Some Factors. 12, 1980-81, pp. 7-15.

Mesolithic-Megalithic Links — New Thoughts for Study in India. 10, 1978-79, pp. 62-65.

Middle Palaeolithic in India. 13 & 14, 1981-83, pp. 9-14.

Protohistoric Indian Metal Tools for Tillage — A Note. 11, 1979-80, pp. 59-64.

Use of Arch in the Kushan Palace at Kausambi. 11, 1979-80, pp. 96-102.

Subbaiah, P.C. Venkata
Protohistoric Investigations in the Central Pennar Basin, Cuddapah District, Andhra Pradesh. 18, 1987-88, pp. 79-84.

Srivastava, Balram
Sankhu Buddha. 1, 1967-68, pp. 85-86.

Srivastava, K.M.
Note on the Recent Excavations at Piprahwa, Distt. Basti. (U.P.) 6, 1972-73, p.51.

Srivastava, Surendra Kumar
Episode from Rāmāyaṇa on a Terracotta Panel. 1, 1967-68, pp. 93-95.

Srivastava, Suryakant
Some More Copper Objects from Sheorajpur. 19, 1988-89, pp. 70-71.

Stacul, G.
On Periods and Cultures in the Swat Valley and Beyond. 10, 1978-79, pp. 89-91.

Sundara, A.
Excavations at Sannati: 1986-87. 17, 1986-87, pp. 22-25.

New Type of Neolithic Burial in Terdal, Mysore State. 3, 1969-70, pp. 23-33.

Place Names, Traditions and Archaeology. 22, 1991-92, pp. 97-101.

Suran, Himanshu Prabha
Anthropomorphic Ornaments in Early Indian Sculpture. 7, 1974, pp. 103-105.

Tandon, B.N.
Environmental Protection for Taj Mahal, Agra and Other Monuments. 11, 1979-80, pp. 160-162.

Tandon, O.P.
Alamgirpur and the Iron Age in India. 1, 1967-68, pp. 54-60.

Thakkar, A.M.
Fallacies of Archaeological Interpretation. 8, 1975-76, pp. 182-183.

Thakur, Vijay Kumar
Archaeology of Early Mediaeval Towns in Bengal. 12, 1980-81, pp. 140-145.

Thapar, B.K.
Archaeology of South Asia: A Perspective in Inter- Relationship. 22, 1991-92, pp. 1-4.

Comments on "Concept on Urban Revolution". 6, 1972-73, pp. 35-36A.

Fresh light on the Neolithic Cultures of India. 13 & 14, 1981-83, pp. 37-43.

Problems of the Neolithic Cultures in India: a Retrospect. 7, 1974, pp. 61-65.

Thapar, Romila
Puranic Lineages and Archaeological Cultures. 8, 1975-76, pp. 86-98.

Thapliyal, Kiran Kumar
'Chandragupta Kumaradevi' Commemorative Medals. 12, 1980-81, pp. 152-154.

Clay Tablet in Lucknow Museum: An Artistic and Religious Study. 1, 1967-68, pp. 90-92.

Harappans and the Aryans. 10, 1978-79, pp. 122-125.

Interesting Sealing from Musanagar. 2, 1968-69, pp. 57-58.

Sealing from Sunet and Śaiva-Vaishṇava Syncretism. 3, 1969-70, pp. 74-76.

Vaishṇava Sealing from Jhusi. 3, 1969-70, p. 53.

Tripathi, Vibha
From Copper to Iron — A Transition. 15, 1984-85, pp. 75-79.

Tripathi, Sila
Ancient Ports of Orissa: Probable causes of their decline. 23, 1992-93, pp. 50-53.

Trivedi, C.B.
Excavations at Kotra. 1988-89. 22, 1991-92, pp. 122-124.

Newly Discovered Gupta Sculptures from Madhya Pradesh. 11, 1979-80, pp. 150-151.

Trivedi, P.K.
Door-Jamb at Kayavarohana: A Reappraisal. 11, 1979-80, pp. 84-87.

Ullah, Sana, Mohd.
Extract from "Ancient India, No. 1" 1946, p. 58–5, 1971-72, p. 59.

Varma, Radha Kant
Mesolithic Cultures of India. 13 & 14, 1981-83, pp. 27-36.

Vasantamadhava, K.V.
Hero Stones in Manki. 23, 1992-93, pp. 84-85.

Verma, B.S.
Excavations at Chirand: New light on the Indian Neolithic Culture-complex. 4, 1970-71, pp. 19-22.

Wahal, L.M.
Session on OCP. 5, 1971-72, pp. 12-13.

Wakanakar, V.S.
New Light on Central Indian Archaeology through Kayatha Excavations. 2, 1968-69, pp. 26-29.

Vikram University, Ujjain (Archaeology in Universities). 2, 1968-69, pp. 65-66.

Walimbe, S.R.
Human Skeletal Remains from Megalithic Vidarbha. 18, 1987-88, pp. 61-71.

Walker, J., Michael and Santoso, S.
Romano-Indian Rouletted Pottery in Indonesia. 9, 1977-78, pp. 104-108.

TITLE INDEX

About the Shortughai Sequence from Mature Harappan to Late Bactrian: Bronze age in Eastern Bactria (N.E. Afghanistan). — **Frankfort, H.P.** 10, 1978-79, pp. 91-94.

Abstract from 'Some Technical Observations on NBP Ware Slip', in Potteries in Ancient India. — **H.C. Bhardwaj.** 5, 1971-72, pp. 62-63.

Abstract from "The Indus Valley Culture" — **Gurdip Singh.** 4, 1970-71, pp. 68-76.

Acheulian Industry of Rock Shelter II F-23 at Bhimbetka, Central India: a Preliminary Study — **V.N. Misra.** 8, 1975-76, pp. 133-36.

Agricultural Remains from Madhya Pradesh (India) from Chalcolithic Period to Mauryan Period — **R.A. Sharma.** 22, 1991-92, pp. 53-58.

Alamgirpur and the Iron Age in India — **O.P. Tandon.** 1, 1967-68, pp. 54-60.

(An) Appraisal of the Protohistoric Problems of the Ganga-Yamuna doab — **R.C. Gaur.** 4, 1970-71, pp. 42-50.

Anangpur: A Plaeolithic Site near Delhi — **A.K. Sharma and S. B. Ota.** 21, 1990-91, pp. 73-74.

Analytical Investigation of Indian Bronzes — **M. Singh.** 21, 1990-91, pp. 96-99.

Ancient Gold Working: Some New ^{14}C Dates— **D.P. Agrawal and C. Margabandhu.** 8, 1975-76, pp. 138-139.

Ancient Indian Pottery- kilns— **K.T.M. Hegde.** 9, 1977-78, pp. 109-111.

Ancient Plant Economy at Inamgaon — **Vishnu Mittre and R. Savithri.** 8, 1975-76, pp. 55-62.

Ancient Plant Economy at Noh, Rajasthan — **Vishnu Mittre and R. Savithri.** 7, 1974, pp. 77-80.

Ancient Ports of Orissa: Probable causes of their decline — **Sila Tripathi.** 23, 1992-93, pp. 50-53.

Animal Bones From Gufkral—Evidence of Human and Non-Human Activities — **A.K. Sharma.** 12, 1980-81, pp. 31-36.

Anthropomorphic Ornaments in Early Indian Sculpture — **Himanshu Prabha Suran.** 7, 1974, pp. 103-105.

An Optimal Modelling Exercise for the Harappan Civilization with Special Reference to its Regional context in Haryana, India — **Vijneshu Mohan.** 23, 1992-93, pp. 13-20.

Antiquity of Gold-Glasses in India. — **Ravindra N. Singh.** 12, 1980-81, pp. 157-159.

Ārambha: a Vakataka site in Vidarbha — **Amarendra Nath.** 22, 1991-92, pp. 69-74.

Archaeology and Indian Tradition: Some Observations — **M.C. Joshi.** 8, 1975-76, pp. 98-102.

Archaeology and the Problem of Regional Identity — **Y.B. Singh.** 12, 1980-81, pp. 150-151.

Archaeology and the Rāmāyaṇa or Dating the Rāmāyaṇa — **H.D. Sankalia.** 1, 1967-68, pp. 1-3.

Archaeology and Tamil Literary Tradition — **R. Champaklakshmi.** 8, 1975-76, pp. 110-122.

Archaeology and Tradition: The Later Vedic Phase and the Painted Grey Ware Culture — **R.S. Sharma.** 8, 1975-76, pp. 63-67.

Archaeology in India Since Independence: Some Random Thoughts — **B.B. Lal.** 12, 1980-81, pp. 15-21.

Archaeology of Early Medieval Towns in Bengal — **Vijay Kumar Thakur.** 12, 1980-81, pp. 140-145.

Archaeology of South Asia: A Perspective in Inter-relationship — **B.K. Thapar.** 22, 1991-92, pp. 1-4.

Archaeology of Thanesar: A Brief Report on Excavations at Harsh-ka-Tila — **B.M. Pande.** 19, 1988-89, pp. 1-5.

Archaeology of the Wardha–Wainganga Divide — **Amarendra Nath.** 20, 1980-90, pp. 93-98.

Archaeological and Ethnographic Evidence for the Hafting and Use of Microliths and Related Tools — **V.N. Misra.** 7, 1974, pp. 3-12.

(The) Archaeological background and iron sample from Hatigra — **N.C. Ghosh, Arun K. Nag, Pranab K. Chattopadhyay.** 18, 1987-88, pp. 21-27.

Archaeological Chemistry in India–Some Aspects — **R.V. Joshi.** 13 & 14, 1981-83, pp. 111-114.

Archaeological Explorations in Basti District (U.P.) — **S.K. Bhatt.** 3, 1969-70, pp. 77-88.

Archaeological findings from Durvasa — **B.C. Shukla.** 16, 1985-86, pp. 33-35.

Archaeological Material from West Bengal in the Zoological Survey of India — **S. Banerjee.** 11, 1979-80, pp. 162-164.

Archaeological Reconnaissance in Birbhum — **Dilip K. Chakrabarti and A. K. Nag.** 10, 1978-89, pp. 25-32.

Archaeological Testimony of Surunga and the Mauryanism of the Arthasastra of Kautilya — **Suresh Chandra Mishra.** 19, 1988-89, pp. 74-76.

Archaeometallurgical study of Iron Pillar at Dhar — **B. Prakash.** 20, 1989-90, pp. 118-122.

Archaeometallurgical studies at Kankrajhor and Dhuliapur — **Sudhin De and Pranab K. Chattopadhyay.** 20, 1989-90, pp. 115-117.

Are the Defences of Kausambi Really as old as 1025 B.C.? — **B.B. Lal.** 11, 1979-80, pp. 88-95.

Armenian Cemetery of Hyderabad — **Mohd. Abdul Waheed Khan.** 6, 1972-73, p. 79.

Art and its Decorative Out look — **Anupa Pande.** 22, 1991-92, pp. 132-133.

(The) Aryans—A Fresh Appraisal — **R.C. Gaur.** 12, 1980-81, pp. 133-135.

At Random — **A. Ghosh.** 8, 1975-76, pp. 123-125.

An Attempt Towards the Interpretation of Rock Paintings at Kethavaram — **N. Chandra Mouli.** 18, 1987-88, pp. 72-78.

Atmospheric Pollution and Cultural Property — **O.P. Agrawal.** 13 & 14, 1981-83, pp. 149-154.

Authors of the Indus Seal Texts or the Indus Seal Motifs — **M.N. Gupta.** 12, 1980-81, pp. 47-53.

Ayodhya and God Rama — **Ajay Mitra Shastri.** 23, 1992-93, pp. 35-39.

Ayodhya: Mythical and Real — **M.C. Joshi.** 11, 1979-80, pp. 107-109.

Ayodhya of the Valmiki Ramayana: An Energizing Debate on its Identification — **B.B. Lal.** 16, 1985-86, pp. 79-86.

Banganga-Beas Palaeolithic Industry: A Look-Back — **B.B. Lal.** 11, 1979-80, pp. 1-10.

Beginning of Iron Age in Garhwal, Mid-Central Himalaya: An Ecological Overview — **Vinod Nautiyal, K.P. Nautiyal, B.M. Khanduri, D.L. Rajput.** 21, 1990-91, pp. 29-35.

Bibliography of OCP and Related Literature. 5, 1971-72, pp. 65-75.

Bibliography of the NBP Ware. 5, 1971-72, pp. 76-83.

Bibliographical Aids for the Study of the Indus Civilization: A Critical Survey — **Asko Parpola.** 8, 1975-76, pp. 150-156.

Biostratigraphy of the Central Narmada Valley with special reference to Hexaprotodon Spp — **Salahuddin.** 18, 1987-88, pp. 1-20.

Black Lustrous Ware of Himachal Pradesh — **A.N. Khanna.** 10, 1978-79, pp. 117-118,

Bone and Antler Industry from Allahapur, District Meerut — **K.N. Dikshit.** 4, 1970-71, pp. 51-55.

Braj Basi Lal. — **Anon.** 13 & 14, 1981-83, vii-viii.

Bronze Age Culture of Thailand — **Mahesh Prasad Madhukar.** 16, 1985-86, pp. 59-62.

Buddhist Relic Caskets in Indian Museums — **S.K. Bhattacharya.** 17, 1986-87, pp. 43-49.

Burial Practices in the Neolithic Cultures of South India — **Purushottam Singh.** 1, 1967-68, pp. 31-35.

Burnt Brick Structure At Hulas — **V.C. Sharma.** 11, 1979-80, pp. 148-149.

Cairn Burials of Baluchistan, Makran and South-east Iran: their Character and Chronology — **K.S. Ramachandran.** 7, 1974, pp. 82-87.

Casing Slab from Nagarjunkonda—A Reappraisal — **Anamika Pathak.** 19, 1988-89, pp. 72-73.

Cemetery 'H' Culture — **H.D. Sankalia.** 6, 1972-73, pp. 12-19.

Ceramics and Maritime Routes of India: New Evidence — **I.K. Sarma.** 21, 1990-91, pp. 37-42.

Chalcolithic Burials: The Tekwada Evidence — **M.K. Dhavalikar.** 2, 1968-69, pp. 35-40.

Chalcolithic Culture: A Socio-Economic Perspective — **M.K. Dhavalikar.** 13 & 14, 1981-83, pp. 63-80.

Chalcolithic Culture of southern Bihar as Revealed by the Exploration and Excavation in District Rohtas — **Birendra Pratap Singh.** 20, 1989-90, pp. 83-92.

'Chandragupta-Kumaradevi' Commemorative Medals — **Kiran Kumar Thapliyal.** 12, 1980-81, pp. 152-154.

Changing Face of Archaeological Studies —**K.V. Soundara Rajan.**1, 1967-68, pp. 24-30.

Channel-Spouted Vessel From Hissar — **Parveen Moghrdam and Dilip K. Chakrabarti.** 8, 1975-76, pp. 164-165.

Chaturmukha Siva-Linga from Nand near Pushkar, Rajasthan — **R.C. Agrawala.** 2, 1968-69, pp. 53-54.

Chemistry of Deccan Chalcolithic Deposits from Daimabad and Inamgaon — **R.V. Joshi, B.C. Deotare, A.A. Kshirsagar.** 10, 1978-79, pp. 80-81.

Chronology of Indian Megaliths—Some Considerations — **K.S. Ramachandran.** 3, 1969-70, pp. 107-109.

Chronology of Mathura—An Assessment — **M.C. Joshi and A.K. Sinha.** 10, 1978-79, pp. 39-44.

Chronology of Painted Grey Ware. Did the Painted Grey Ware continue up to the Mauryan Times? — **B.B. Lal.** 9, 1977-78, pp. 64-80.

Clay tablet in Lucknow Museum: An Artistic and Religious Study — **Kiran Kumar Thapliyal.** 1, 1967-68, pp. 90-92.

Coins and Small Finds of Indian Origin in Ai-Khanum (Afghanistan) — **O. Gulliaume.** 16, 1985-86, pp. 87-88.

Comments on C.C. Lamberg-Karlovsky's paper on 'Trade Mechanisms in Indus-Mesopotamian Interrelations' — **Dilip K. Chakrabarti.** 7, 1974, pp. 74-75.

Comments on "Concept of Urban Revolution",— **M.C. Joshi.** 6, 1972-73, p. 36 B.

Comments on "Concept of Urban Revolution....", — **N.R. Banerjee.** 6, 1972-73, pp. 32-33.

Comments on "Concept of Urban Revolution", — **A. Ghosh.** 6, 1972-73, pp. 34-35.

Comments on "Concept of Urban Revolution", — **Krishna Deva.** 6, 1972-73, pp. 33-34.

Comments on "Concept on Urban Revolution", — **B.K. Thapar.** 6, 1972-73, pp. 35-36A.

Comments on Heliodorus Pillar at Besnagar — **M.D. Khare.** 8, 1975-76, pp. 176-178.

Comments on Painted Grey Ware Culture — **K.N. Dikshit.** 9, 1977-78, pp. 81-83.

Comments on Subsistence Pattern of an Early Farming Community of Western India — **Y.M. Chitalwala.** 8, 1975-76, p. 140.

Composite Images of Lakshmi and Vishnu: Some Observations — **M.C. Joshi.** 11, 1979-80, pp. 81-83.

Compoundable Prosodic signs in the Indus Script — **M.N. Gupta.** 10, 1978-79, pp. 109-115.

Concept of Urban Revolution and the Indian Context — **Dilip K. Chakrabarti.** 6, 1972-73, pp. 27-32.

"Copper Hoards" from West Bengal — **A.K. Nag and Dilip K. Chakrabarti.** 9, 1977-78, pp. 97-99.

Copper Hoard Culture of India: A Reasessment — **Makkhan Lal.** 12, 1980-81, pp. 65-77.

Copper Hoard Implements in the National Museum, New Delhi: 1987 Collection — **D.P. Sharma.** 17, 1986-87, pp. 38-42.

"Coper Hoard" Implements in the National Museum Collection: 1986 — **S.P. Gupta.** 16, 1985-86, pp. 45-46.

Copper Red Glasses through the Ages — **H.C. Bhardwaj.** 3, 1969-70, pp. 2-8.

Credit and Mortgage Documents in the *Lekhapaddhati* — **Pushpa Prasad.** 18, 1987-88, pp. 93-101.

Crystal Human-figure from Sonepur — **B.P. Sinha.** 2, 1968-69, pp. 51-52.

Cult Object on Unicorn Seals: A Sacred filter? — **Iravatham Mahadevan.** 13 & 14, 1981-83, pp. 165-186.

Culture and Process — **Gregory L. Possehl.** 9, 1977-78, pp. 43-46.

Daimabad—A Rediscovery — **M.K. Dhavalikar.** 3, 1969-70, pp. 34-43.

Dangwada (Ujjain)—A Chalcolithic Site — **M.D. Khare.** 11, 1979-80, pp. 117-120.

Date of King Dhanadeva of Kosala: A Re-Examiantion of the Palaeographic and Historical Evidence — **B.B. Lal and K.K. Sharma.** 19, 1988-89, pp. 38-42.

Deccan College Post-Graduate and Research Institute, Poona (Archaeology in Universities Series) — **H.D. Sankalia.** 2, 1968-69, p. 60.

Defence System in Ancient India based on Literary and Archaeological Evidence — **V.C. Sharma.** 21, 1990-91, pp. 65-69.

Deogarh Acheulian Assemblage: A Preliminary Report — **Makkhan Lal and Salahuddin.** 20, 1989-90, pp. 65-70.

Depiction of Cattle Motifs on Amri Pottery (A comparative study with Baluchistan) — **Poonam Chitkara.** 9, 1977-78, pp. 92-96.

Determining the Techniques of Handmade and Wheel-turned pottery by Microscopic Analysis — **S. P. Gupta.** 2, 1968-69, pp. 23-35.

Development of Early Śaiva Art: Indian Architecture with Special Reference to Andhra Pradesh — **S.P. Gupta.** 11, 1979-80, p. 173.

Development of Sculptural Stone and Terracotta Art in India from the Beginning to the Mauryan Age — **R.C. Sharma.** 22, 1991-92, pp. 65-68.

Dholavira: A New Horizon of the Indus Civilization — **R.S. Bisht.** 20, 1989-90, pp. 71-82.

Discovery of an Early Inscription from Pitalkhora — **S.K. Mitra.** 21, 1990-91, pp. 84-85.

Discovery of Lithic Artifacts in Jammu Area — **G.C. Mohapatra and Hari Mohan Saroj.** 2, 1962-69, pp. 11-12.

Discovery of Ochre Coloured Pottery from Noh, District Bharatpur — **Vijaya Kumar.** 5, 1971-72, pp. 43-44.

(The) Distribution and Types of Beads in the Gangetic Valley — **S. Jamal Hasan.** 11, 1979-80, pp. 131-140.

Distribution of Painted Grey Ware Sites in District Bharatpur (Rajasthan) — **B.S. Negi.** 12, 1980-81, pp. 129-132.

Domestic Animals in the Early Cultures of India — **Roswitha Conrad.** 7, 1974, pp. 76-77.

Domestic Art Delineated in the Gandhara Reliefs — **K. Kirhsna Murthy.** 7, 1974, pp. 96-103.

Door-jamb at Kayavarohana: A Reappraisal — **P.K. Trivedi.** 11, 1979-80, pp. 84-87.

Dots, Cup-marks and Pits vis-a-vis the Megaliths—New Evidences from Kumaon — **Maheshwar P. Joshi.** 16, 1985-86, pp. 25-28.

Drawing in Archaeology: Suggestions — **S.S. Saar.** 10, 111978-79, pp. 115-117.

Dynmaics of Pre-Harappan Cultures — **Shashi Asthana.** 13 & 14, 1981-83, pp. 45-50.

Early Farming Communities of Kaimur Foot-hills — **Birendra Pratap Singh.** 19, 1988-89, pp. 6-18.

Early Harappan Culture-phase: A Reply — **Rafique Mughal.** 9, 1977-78, pp. 84-87.

Early Historic Fortifications in the Ganga Valley — **Madhukar Shripad Mate.** 3, 1969-70, pp. 58-69.

Early Historical Urban Growth in India: Some Observations — **M.C. Joshi.** 7, 1974, pp. 90-91.

Early Representations of Buddha and Buddhist Traditions in *Aśokāvadāna* — **M.C. Joshi.** 21, 1990-91, pp. 1-6.

Early Temple in Gujarat—Excavations at Gojra (Mahadevpura) — **B.M. Pande and Narayan Vyas.** 20, 1989-90, pp. 107-110.

Early Warehouse on the Western-Coast — **M.K. Dhavalikar.** 9, 1977-78, pp. 100-103.

Eco-Functional Frame of Early Man—Some Factors — **K.V. Soundara Rajan.** 12, 1980-81, pp. 7-15.

Economic Pattern of India during the Early Iron Age (1000 B.C.-100 A.D.) Gujarat — **R.N. Mehta.** 9, 1977-80, pp. 52-55.

Environmental Protection for Taj Mahal, Agra and other Monuments — **B.N. Tandon.** 11, 1979-80, pp. 160-162.

Episode from Rāmāyaṇa on a Terracotta Panel — **Surendra Kumar Srivastava.** 1, 1967-68, pp. 93-95.

Ethno-Archaeology of the Traditional Ceremonial Pottery of Gujarat — **Syed Anis Hashim.** 19, 1988-89, pp. 60-63.

Ethnoarchaeological Survey on Ceramic Production — **Valentine Roux.** 16, 1985-86, pp. 63-64.

Evidence of Horse from the Harappan Settlement at Surkotada— **A.K. Sharma.** 7, 1974, pp. 75-76.

Evidence of Social Differentiation and Socio-Political Organisation during the Megalithic Period in South India — **Udairavi S. Moorti.** 20, 1989-90, pp. 1-64.

Excavations at Baharia, District Shahjahanpur — **G.R. Sharma.** 5, 1971-72, pp. 42-43.

Excavations at Chirand: New light on the Indian Neolithic Culture-Complex — **B.S. Verma.** 4, 1970-71, pp. 19-22.

Excavations at Daulatpur (District Bulandshahar) and its Significance — **R.C. Gaur.** 17, 1986-87, p. 56.

Excavations at Golabi Sasan, District Puri, Orissa — **B.K. Sinha.** 21, 1990-91, pp. 74-76.

Excavations at Golabi Sasan, District Puri, Orissa — **B.K. Sinha.** 23, 1992-93, pp. 48-50.

Excavations at Gufkral-1981 — **A.K. Sharma.** 11, 1979-80, pp. 19-25.

Excavations at Hatikara: a Chalcolthicc site in West Bengal — **N.C. Ghosh and S. Nag.** 15, 1984-85, pp. 116.

Excavations at Imlidih Khurd — **Purushottam Singh, Ashok Kumar Singh and Indrajeet Singh.** 22, 1991-92, pp. 120-122.

Excavations at Karkabhat — **A.K. Sharma.** 21, 1990-91, pp. 21-24.

Excavations at Kotra 1988-89 — **C.B. Trivedi.** 22, 1991-92, pp. 122-

Excavations at Ladyura, Almora, U.P.— **A.K. Sharma.** 21, 1990-91, pp. 77-79.

Excavations at Lalkot 1991-92 and Further Exploration in Delhi — **B.R. Mani.** 22. 1991-92, pp. 75-87.

Excavations at Manjhi 1983-85: A Preliminary Report— **T.N. Roy.** 16, 1985-86, pp. 29-32.

Excavation at Moradhwaj—A note — **K.P. Nautiyal and B.M. Khanduri.** 10, 1978-79, pp. 86-87.

Excavations at Narhan 1983-85— **Purushottam Singh, Makkhan Lal and Ashok Kumar Singh.** 15, 1984-85, pp. 117-120.

Excavation at Rohira — **G.B. Sharma and Manmohan Kumar.** 12, 1980-81, pp. 125-127.

Excavations at Rojdi: 1982-83 — **Gregory L. Possehl, Y.M. Chitalwala, Paul Rissman and Gail Wagner.** 13 & 14 1981-83, pp. 155-163.

Excavations at Sannati: 1986-87 — **A. Sundara.** 17, 1986-87, pp. 22-25.

Excavation at Taradih — **Ajit Kumar Prasad.** 12, 1980-81, pp. 138-139.

Excavation at Vadagokugiri (Meghalaya) 1992 — **A.K. Sharma.** 22, 1991-92, pp. 89-96

Excavation at Zekhada — **K.N. Momin.** 12, 1980-81, pp. 120-125.

Excavations of an Apsidal Brick Temple at Banavasi, District North Canara — **M. Seshadri.** 4, 1970-71, pp. 56-57.

Excavations of a Vedic Brick Altar at Purola, District Uttar Kashi, Central Himalaya — **K.P. Nautiyal and B.M. Khanduri.** 19, 1988-89, pp. 68-69.

Exploration Reveals a fresh Light on the History of Kisan Bilas, District Kota, Rajasthan.— **S.C. Saran.** 12, 1980-81, pp. 148-150.

Explorations along the Banganga River, District Bharatpur, Rajasthan — **Baldev Singh Negi.** 17, 1986-87, pp. 5-10.

Explorations along the Sahibi River in District Gurgaon — **C. Margabandhu and R.P. Sharma.** 10, 1978—79, pp. 14-19.

Explorations of Prehistoric Sites in District Bijapur — **R.S. Pappu.** 4, 1970-71, pp. 58-62.

Exposing and Conserving a World Heritage Monument — **A.K. Sharma.** 19, 1988-89, pp. 64-67.

Extract from Ancient India No. 1, New Delhi. 1946, p. 58 — **Mohd. Sana Ullah.** 5, 1971-72, p. 59.

Extract from Current Science, December 20, 1966, 35, No. 24, p. 623 — **K.T.M. Hegde.** 5, 1971-72, pp. 62.

Extract from Indian Archaeology—A Review, 1955-56, pp. 56-57 — **B.B. Lal.** 5. 1971-72, p. 61.

Extract from Indian Archaeology—A Review, 1959-60, pp. 120-121 — **B.B. Lal.** 5, 1971-72, p. 61.

Extract from R.E.M. Wheeler's "Early India and Pakistan", London, 1959, p. 30 — **Ms. Bimson.** 5, 1971-72, pp. 61-62.

Extracts from 'Physics and Chemistry in Indian Archaeology' Paper read at the annual conference, Indian Archaeological Society, Nagpur, 1970 — **K.T.M. Hegde.** 5, 1971-72, pp. 63-64.

Extracts from 'The Surface Treatment of Early Indian Pottery', *Man* 1953, Art 58, pp. 41-42 — **P.S. Rawson.** 5, 1971-72, pp. 59-60.

Fallacies of Archaeological Interpretation — **A.M. Thakkar.** 8, 1975-76, pp. 182-183.

Fresh light on the Neolithic Cultures of India — **B.K. Thapar.** 13 & 14, 1981-83, pp. 37-43.

From Copper to Iron—A Transition — **Vibha Tripathi.** 15, 1984-85, pp. 75-79.

Functional Significance of the O.C.P. and P.G.W. Shapes and Associated Objects — **H.D. Sankalia.** 7, 1974, pp. 47-52.

Further Light on Lower Paleolithic Occupation and Palaeoenvironment in Semi-arid Zone of Rajasthan — **V.N. Misra, S.N. Rajaguru, R.J. Wasson, G. Singh, and D.P. Agrawal.** 11, 1979-80, pp. 11-18.

Further note on the Direction of Writing in the Harappan Script — **B.B. Lal.**1, 1967-68, pp. 15-16.

Ganeshwar Culture—An Appraisal — **K.N. Dikshit and A.K. Sinha.** 11, 1979-80, pp. 120-122.

Genesis of Harappa Culture — **D.P. Agrawal.** 6, 1972-73, pp. 37-41.

Glazed Ware in India — **K.K. Mohammad.** 15, 1984-85, pp. 105-110.

Greek or Yavana Donors in Ancient India — **S.D. Dogra.** 8, 1975-76, pp. 185-190.

Grey Ware Culture of Northern Pakistan, Jammu & Kashmir and Panjab — **T.N. Khazanchi and K.N. Dikshit.** 9, 1977-78, pp. 47-51.

Gulf of Oman: the Original Home of Indian Megaliths — **S.P. Gupta.** 4, 1970-71, pp. 4-8.

Gulf of Oman: Original Home of the Indian Megaliths A Reappraisal — **K.S. Ramachandran.** 6, 1972-73, pp. 20-26.

Handaxe and Chopper-Chopping Tool Tradition: the Idea of Two Culture Theory of Early Palaeolithic in Asia — **A.P. Khatri.** 9, 1977-78, pp. 3-14.

Harappa Culture: Emergence of a New Picture — **Jagat Pati Joshi.** 13 & 14, 1981-83, pp. 51-54.

Harappan and Rigvedic Inter-relations — **Malati Shendge.** 8, 1975-76, pp. 103-110.

Harappan and Vedic Civilization: An Analysis of Legacy — **K.D. Bajpei.** 20, 1991-92, pp. 115-117.

Harappan Chronology: an Integrated Study — **S.B. Ray.** 7, 1974, pp. 65-69.

Harappan Furnaces — **D.V. Sharma.** 11, 1979-80, pp. 125-127.

Harappan Horned Deity: The evidence from Padri in Western India — **Vasant Shinde.** 21, 1990-91, pp. 79-81.

Harappans and the Aryans — **K.K. Thapliyal.** 10, 1978-79, pp. 122-125.

Harappans in Saurashtra: New Chronological Considerations — **Gregory L. Possehl.** 22, 1991-92, pp. 25-29.

(The) Heliodorus Pillar at Besnagar - **John Irwin.** 8, 1975-76, pp. 166-76.

Herding as the Backdrop to the Growth of Agriculture in West Asia and South Asia — **S.P. Gupta and Arun Kesarwani.** 12, 1980-81, pp. 101-111.

Hero Stones in Manki — **K.V. Vasantamadhava.** 23, 1992-93, pp. 84-85.

Highlights of the International Symposium on Radio-carbon and Indian Archaeology-1972 — **S.P. Gupta, P.C. Pant, K.N. Dikshit and B.M. Pande.** 6, 1972-73, pp. 80-83.

Historical Archaeology: Review and Perspective— **S.B. Deo.**13 & 14, 1981-83, pp. 87-95.

Historical Urbanization—A Suggestive Date — **A.K. Sinha.** 11, 1979-80, pp. 151-155.

Human Settlements in Goa till 16th Century: An overview — **S.K. Joshi.** 23, 1992-93, pp. 63-64.

Human Skeletal Remains from Megalithic Vidarbha — **S.R. Walimbe.** 18, 1987-88, pp. 61-71.

Identification of Pundravardhana— **Achyutanand Jha.** 21, 1990-91, pp. 81-84.

Identification of Setavya, the Ancient City of Kosala with Siswania and its Terracotta Art — **B.R. Mani.** 21, 1990-91, pp. 43-49.

Identification of Soma — **Bhagwan Singh.** 12, 1980-81, pp. 154-157.

Indian Archaeology and the Epic Traditions — **B.D. Chattopadhyaya.** 8, 1975-76, pp. 67-72.

Indian Archaeology, A Review: Guide to Excavated Sites: 1953-54 through 1984-85 — **Gregory L. Possehl.** 18, 1987-88, pp. 113-171.

Indian Civilisation: the Formative Period; Indian Instt. of Advanced Study, Simla, 1968 — **D.P. Agrawal.** 4, 1970-71, pp. 63-65.

Indian Indonesia — **C.C. Mullick.** 17, 1986-87, pp. 33-37.

Indian Tradition and Archaeology — **B.P. Sinha.**13 & 14, 1981-83, pp. 103-109.

Indo-Aryan Rulers oi Ancient Western Asia and their Documents — **Jamna Das Akhtar.** 10, 1978-79, pp. 66-69.

Indus Civilization–Echoes in later Literature — **Y.B. Singh.**16, 1985-86, pp. 15-16.

Indus Culture Seal of Three Forms and Seven Figures as Pictorial Representation of AV Hymn IV. 37 — **P.V. Pathak.** 22, 1991-92, pp. 59-63.

Indus Sealing from Hulas — **Iravatham Mahadevan.** 11, 1979-80, p. 117.

Indus Valley Civilization–An Aryan culture?— **P.B. Bhattacharya.** 11, 1979-80, pp. 140-145.

Inscribed Copper Tablets from Mohenjo-daro: Some Observations — **B.M. Pande.** 21, 1990-91, pp. 25-28.

Inscribed Harappan Material from Kalibangan: Some Remarks on Methodology and Approach — **B.M. Pande.** 8, 1975-76, pp. 156-157.

Inscribed Harappan potsherds from Chandigarh — **B.M. Pande.** 6, 1972-73, pp. 52-55.

Interesting Sealing from Musanagar — **Kiran Kumar Thapliyal.** 2, 1968-69, pp. 57-58.

Interpretation of Function of Microlithic tool (Lunate) through Microwear Examination — **Gayatri Chaturvedi.** 22, 1991-92, pp. 5-12.

Inter-relations between Archaeology and Plant Sciences — **Vishnu Mittre.** 1, 1967-68, pp. 4-14.

Iron Age and Peninsular India — **K.N. Dikshit.** 22, 1991-92, pp. 31-34.

Iron and Gemstone Industries as Revealed from Kodumanal Excavations — **K. Rajan.** 20, 1989-90, pp. 111-112.

Iron and Urbanization: an Examination of the Indian Context — **Dilip K. Chakrabarti.** 15, 1984-85, pp. 68-74.

Iron at Ahar: A Comment — **Makkhan Lal.** 18, 1987-88, pp. 109-112.

Is the early Pottery from Kausambi Harappan? — **K.N. Dikshit.** 11, 1979-80, pp. 103-105.

Ivory and Bone Plaquettes—A Note — **A.K. Sinha.** 10, 1978-79, pp. 101-103.

Jain Vestiges at Renukonda Fort — **A. Gurumurthi.** 22, 1991-92, pp. 103-107.

Jamalpur: A Typological Variant within the Middle Palaeolithic Culture-complex of India — **P.C. Pant and Vidula Jayaswal.** 9, 1977-78, pp. 15-33.

Kamauli Copper Plate Inscription of Govindachandra (Vikram Year 1197) — **A.K. Singh.** 22, 1991-92, pp. 117-120.

Kameśvara Temple at Galiavalli — **M. Krishnakumari.** 16, 1985-86, pp. 55-58.

Kashmir—Where the Roots of Western Tibetan Art lie — **A.K. Singh.** 12, 1980-81, pp. 145-148.

Khairadih—a Chalcolithic settlement — **Birendra Pratap Singh.** 18, 1987-88, pp. 28-34.

Khaparkhera: A Submergible Chalcolithic Site — **S.B. Ota.** 21, 1990-91, pp. 76-77.

Khatoli—A Protohistoric site in Haryana — **R.P. Sharma.** 11, 1979-80, pp. 123-125.

Knapping Technique and Craft Specialization: An Ethnoarchaelogical Investigation in Gujarat — **Valentine Roux and Jacques Pelegrin.** 19, 1988-89, pp. 50-59.

Kshetrapala shrine at Kandhar — **M.K. Dhavalikar and A.P. Jamkhedkar.** 20, 1989, pp. 99-106.

Laboratory Studies in the Jokha Midden Soil Samples — **Karunakara T.M. Hegde.** 3, 1969-70, pp. 9-14.

Lady of Beasts: The Harappan Goddess — **Shubhangana Atre.** 16, 1985-86, pp. 7-13.

Lady of the Beasts or the Lord of the Beasts: A Reappriasal — **P.V. Pathak.** 21, 1990-91, pp. 57-64.

Lalapur: An Acheulian Site in District Banda (U.P.) — **J.N. Pandey.** 11, 1979-80, pp. 113-116.

Land–use pattern during Chalcolithic period in the Tapi Basin — **Vasant Shinde.** 18, 1987-88, pp. 54-60.

Late Harappan Culture—A Reappraisal — **K.N. Dikshit.** 13 & 14, 1981-83, pp. 55-61.

Later Vedic Phase and the Painted Grey Ware culture — **R. S. Sharma.** 8, 1975-76, pp. 63-67.

Legacy of Indus Civilization in North India — **K.N. Dikshit.** 21, 1990-91, pp. 17-20.

List of Life Members of Indian Archaeological Society. 19, 1988-89, pp. 96-101.

Lithic Industries of Bankura — **Dilip K. Chakrabarti, D.K. Bhattacharya and R.K. Chattopadhyay.** 11, 1979-80, pp. 39-48.

Locating the Graves at Kalibangan — **A.K. Sharma.** 9, 1977-78, pp. 89-91.

Location of Pava — **K.D. Bajpai.** 16, 1985-86, pp. 39-44.

Longer Chronology of the Indus–Saraswati Civilization — **S.P. Gupta.** 23, 1992-93, pp. 21-29.

Lower Palaeolithic in India — **G.C. Mohapatra.** 13 & 14, 1981-83, pp. 1-8.

Mahamrityunjaya in art — **A. Gurumurthi.** 18, 1987-88, pp. 102-105.

Mahāparinirvāṇa Panel in the National Museum Collection — **Shashi Asthana.** 16, 1985-86, pp. 35-37.

Maltese Cross on Protohistoric Pottery — **Madhu Bala.** 11, 1979-80, pp. 129-131.

Mammalian Fossil Fauna: a most Modern Tool for dating the Pleistocene Deposits — **E. Khan.** 4, 1970-71, pp. 31-41.

Medieaval Archaeology — **R.N. Mehta.** 13 & 14, 1981-83, pp. 97-102.

Meeting of the World Archaeological Congress: Steering Committee held at the Cumanagoto Hotel, Cumana, Venezuela on 19 & 20 October 1987. 17, 1986-87, pp. 65-70.

Meeting of the World Archaeological Congress Executive held at the University of South Dakota, Vermillion, USA on 6 August 1989. 19, 1988-89, pp. 84-95.

Megalithic Culture in North Arcot Region — **K. Rajan.** 22, 1991-92, pp. 35-46.

Megalithic Remains in the Aravallis — **Purushottam Singh.** 2, 1968-69, pp. 46-48.

Megaliths in Yemen Arab Republic — **A. Ghosh.** 7, 1974, pp. 81-82.

Mesolithic Cultures of India — **Radha Kant Varma.** 13 & 14, 1981-83, pp. 27-36.

Mesolithic Human Remains from the Gangetic plain Sarai Nahar Rai — **Kennedy, K.A.R., Cristopher B. Burrow, and Nacy C. Lovell.** 15, 1984-85, p. 1-55.

Mesolithic Megalithic Links—New Thoughts for Study in India — **K.V. Soundara Rajan.** 10, 1978-79, pp. 62-65.

Metal Technology of the Indian Protohistoric Cultures: Its Archaeological Implications — **D.P. Agrawal.** 3, 1969-70, pp. 15-22.

Metrical Analysis of Handaxes from Chirki-on-Pravara (Western Maharashtra, India) — **R.V. Joshi, and A.R. Marathe.** 8, 1975-76, pp. 3-12.

Microlithic site from Shahabad (Bihar) — **Bhupendra Pal Singh.** 1, 1967-68, pp. 100-103.

Microlithic Industry of Damdama-Pratapgarh, U.P.: A Preliminary Analysis — **J.N. Pal.** 16, 1985-86, pp. 1-5.

Microliths Around Santiniketan — **D.K. Bhattacharya, Sima Chakrabarti, Dilip K. Chakrabarti.** 10, 1978-79, pp. 83-86.

Middle Palaeolithic in India — **K.V. Soundara Rajan.** 13 & 14, 1981-83, pp. 70-73.

Middle Stone Age Stie on River Durgawati in district Shahabad, Bihar — **Bhupendra Pal Singh** . 3, 1969-70, pp. 70-73.

(A) Model for Understanding the First Urbanization in India — **S.P. Gupta.** 6, 1972-73, pp. 42-50.

Mossbuaer Studies of Black Slipped and Northern Black Polished Wares — **S. Rai and T.N. Roy.** 12, 1980-81, pp. 165-167.

Music and Musical Instrument in Indian Rock-Art — **Erwin Neumayer.** 23, 1992-93, pp. 69-83.

Nageshwar, an Industrial Centre of Chalcolithic Period — **Kuldeep K. Bhan and J.M. Kenoyer.** 12, 1980-81, pp. 115-120.

Nateśa Sculptures in the Early Art of Central India — **Sudha Malaiya.** 16, 1985-86, pp. 47-54.

Neo-Chalcolithic remains at Rangai (Vidisha) — **M.D. Khare.** 12, 1980-81, pp. 55-57.

Neolithic Burial from T. Narasipur — **M. Seshadri.** 2, 1968-69, pp. 55-56.

Neolithic of Western Sub-Himalaya — **G.C. Mohapatra.** 10, 1978-79, pp. 20-24.

New Archaeology and the Indian Situation — **Dhavalikar, M.K.** 10, 1978-79, pp. 33-38.

New Evidence from Kolhua Pillar — **Kalyan Priya Gupta.** 11, 1979-80, pp. 145-147.

New Evidence of Hinayana Buddhism in Vidarbha — **S.B. Deo.** 6, 1972-73, pp. 84-86.

New Gupta Inscription from Kausambi — **B.C. Shukla.** 16, 1985-86, pp. 85-86.

New Light on Central Indian Archaeology through Kayatha Excavations — **V.S. Wakankar.** 2, 1968-69, pp. 26-29.

New Light on Jhusi culture in Allahabad, U.P — **R.S. Rana.** 17, 1986-87, p. 60.

New Light on Vengipura: Excavations at the Ancient Historical City of Andhradesa — **I.K. Sarma.** 17, 1986-87, pp. 15-21.

New Painted Pottery from Vidarbha — **S.B. Deo**. 1, 1967-68, pp. 36-38.

(A) New Tool-Type of the 'Copper Hoards' — **S.P. Gupta.** 11, 1979-80, pp. 127-128.

New Type of Neolithic Burial in Terdal, Mysore State — **A. Sundara.** 3, 1969-70, pp. 23-33.

Newly Discovered Gupta Sculptures from Madhya Pradesh — **C.B. Trivedi.** 11, 1979-80, pp. 150-151.

Northern Black Polished and other Associated wares from Ropar — **K.C. Nauriyal.** 21, 1990-91, pp. 87-89.

Note on a Knot Design from Mohenjo-Daro and its Occurrence in Later Times — **H. Sarkar and B.M. Pande.** 3, 1969-70, pp. 44-48.

Note on Aguncha, District Bhilwara, Rajasthan —**B.L. Nagarch and P.K. Trivedi.** 10, 1976-79, p. 1106.

Note on 'Archaeology of Early Mediaeval Towns in Bengal'— **B.N. Mukherjee.** 15, 1984-85, pp. 121-122.

Note on the Antiquity of Seal — **P.K. Agrawal.** 8, 1975-76, p. 141.

Note on Cross-Contacts of Vedic India with West Asia and Iran — **S.B. Roy.** 8, 1975-76, pp. 146-150.

Note on Makara Figurines — **T.N. Roy.** 3, 1969-70, pp. 105-106.

Note on Pindibandha–An Ancient Dance-form — **Anupa Pande.** 18, 1987-88, pp. 89-92.

Note on Some Ancient Indian Mirrors — **C. Margbandhu.** 7, 1974, pp. 94-95.

Note on the Chemical Composition of some Glass Beads from Rajghat, Varanasi — **H.C. Bhardwaj.** 1, 1967-68, pp. 42-46.

(A) Note on the Excavation at Bhagwanpura — **J.P. Joshi.** 8, 1975-76, pp. 178-180.

(A) Note on the Excavation at Saipai — **B.B. Lal.** 5, 1971-72, pp. 46-49.

(A) Note on the Excavation at Virbhadra — **N.C. Ghosh and R.P. Sharma.** 8, 1975-76, pp. 180-181.

Note on the influence of raw Material on Blank-DetachingTechniques — **Vidula Jayaswal.** 6, 1972-73, pp. 64-70.

Note on the National Museum, Bahrain — **K.N. Dikshit.** 12, 1980-81, pp. 163-1164.

Note on the Recent Excavations at Piprahwa, Distt., Basti (U.P.) — **K.M. Srivastava.** 6, 1972-73, p. 51.

Note on the Stucco figure of Jambhala from Amaravati in Andhra Pradesh — **K. Krishna Murty.** 6, 1972-73, pp. 76-78.

Note on the Treatment of an excavated Iron Object — **O.P. Agrawal and V.C. Sharma.** 11, 1979-80, pp. 159-160.

Numismatics and Archaeology — **Parmeshwari Lal Gupta.** 18, 1987-88, pp. 85-88.

Ochre-Coloured Pottery — A Geochronological Study — **B.B. Lal.** 5, 1971-72, pp. 49-58.

On Flake–blade Element in India — **Ashok K. Ghosh and Dipankar Chaudhury.** 19, 1988-89, pp. 31-37.

On Periods and Cultures in the Swat Valley and Beyond — **G. Stacul.** 10, 1978-79, pp. 89-91.

On the Calibration of C^{14} Dates — **D.P. Agrawal and Sheela Kusumgar.** 7, 1974, pp. 70-73.

On the Conquest of Meluhha by Rimus (2315-2307 B.C.): a Hypothesis — **H. Sarkar.** 8, 1975-76, pp. 157-158.

On the Decipherment of the Indus Script by Soviet Scholars — **Hem Chandra Pande.** 21, 1990-91, pp. 71-72.

On the Identification of Bhakti Deities in Rock Pictures — **Erwin Neumayer.** 23, 1992-93, pp. 53-60.

On the Origin of the Harappan Sign — **B.M. Pande.** 7, 1974, pp. 25-33.

On Tughluq Architecture of Gujarat — **W.H. Siddiqui.** 11, 1979-80, pp. 155-158.

Origin of the Form of Harappan Culture: a New Proposition.— **S.P. Gupta.** 8, 1975-76, pp. 141-146.

Ornithology in Protohistoric Archaeology of India — **V.V. Rao.** 6, 1972-73, pp. 56-59.

Outlines of the Archaeology of Nepal — **N.R. Banerjee.** 2, 1968-69, pp. 1-10.

Painted Grey Ware Culture in Garhwal, Himalaya: New Evidence and Interpretation — **K.P. Nautiyal, B.M. Khanduri, Vinod Nautiyal, D.L. Rajput, and R.K. Bhatt.** 17, 1986-87, pp. 11-14.

Pariar—An Eastern Outpost of the Painted Grey Ware — **B.B. Lal, and K.N. Dikshit.** 11, 1979-80, pp. 26-31.

Parihati, a Mediaeval Smelting Site in Midhapur District, West Bengal — **Dilip K. Chakrabarti and R.K. Chattopadhyay.** 12, 1980-81, pp. 161-163.

Patapadụ Revisited: A New Painted Pottery Culture of South-East India— **I. Karthikeya Sarma.**1, 1967-68, pp. 68-84.

Pella: Where Alexander the Great was Born — **S.D. Dogra.** 7, 1974, pp. 106-107.

Perhaps the Earliest Ploughed Field so far Excavated Anywhere in the World — **B.B. Lal.** 4, 1970-71, pp. 1-3.

Place Names, Traditions and Archaeology —**A. Sundara.** 22, 1991-92, pp. 97-101.

Plant Economy in Ancient Sringverapura Phase-I (C. 1050-1000 B.C.)— **K.S. Saraswat.** 12, 1980-81, pp. 79-80.

Plant Economy of Late Harappans at Hulas — **K.S. Saraswat.** 23, 1992-93, pp. 1-12.

Plant Remains from Ancient Bhatkuli, District Amraoti, Maharashtra — **Vishnu Mittre and H.P. Gupta.** 2, 1968-69, pp. 21-22.

Pleistocene Fossil Vertebrates in India— **G.L. Badam.** 13 & 14, 1981-83, pp. 123-137.

Pollen Analysis and Chemical Examination of a Prehistoric Lake Site at Damdama — **M.D. Kajale and B.C. Deotare.** 19, 1988-89, pp. 27-30.

Pollen Stratigraphy of India — **Vishnu Mittre, Chhaya Sharma, A.K. Saxena, Kamla Prasad, A. Bhattacharya and M.S. Chauhan.** 13 & 14, 1981-83, pp. 115-122.

Population Distribution and its Movement during the Second and First millennia B.C. in the Indo-Gangetic Divide and Upper Ganga plain — **Makkhan Lal.** 18, 1987-88, pp. 35-53.

Pre-Harappans in Punjab — **Y.D. Sharma.** 11, 1979-80, pp. 32-38.

Pre-Harappan Pottery from Distt. Saharanpur (U.P.) — **Shankar Nath.** 11, 1979-80, pp. 122.

Prehistoric Archaeological Studies in Manipur — **M. Jitendra Singh.** 12, 1980-81, pp. 114-115.

Prehistoric Bronze Anthropomorph in the Patna Museum and its Identification — **Prithvi Kumar Agrawala.** 1, 1967-68, pp. 96-98.

Prehistoric Colonization in India: Archaeological and Literary Evidence— **H.D. Sankalia.** 8, 1975-76, pp. 72-86.

Prehistoric Explorations in Sikkim — **A.K. Sharma.** 10, 1978-79, pp. 82-83.

Prehistoric Investigation in the Gambheeram Valley: Visakhapatnam Coast — **P. Vijaya Prakash.** 11, 1979-80, pp. 109-113.

Prehistoric Research in India: As viewed by Two Senior American Archaeologists — **K. Paddayya.** 19, 1988-89, pp. 77-79.

Prehistoric Uttar Pradesh: A Rejoinder to the Review — **P.C. Pant.** 12, 1980-81, pp. 167-169.

Prehistory of Dadra and Nagar Haveli — **W.H. Siddiqui.** 10, 1978-79, pp. 87-89.

Pre-industrial Mines of India — **Dilip K. Chakrabarti.** 16, 1985-86, pp. 65-71.

Problem of Ancient Indian Chronology — **P.L. Bhargava.** 10, 1978-79, pp. 118-122.

Problems of Indian Archaeology: Planning Ahead— **B.B. Lal.** 8, 1975-76, pp. 126-131.

Problems of the Neolithic Culture in India: a Retrospect — **B.K. Thapar.** 7, 1974, pp. 61-65.

Prof. Thieme's Etymology of Skt. 'asi' and its Bearing on the Iron-Age in India — **M.A. Mehendale.** 10, 1978-79, pp. 79-80.

Protohistoric Chronology and Technology and Ecological Factors: A synthesis — **D.P. Agrawal.** 1, 1967-68, pp. 17-23.

Protohistoric Indian Metal Tools for Tillage: A Note — **K.V. Soundara Rajan.** 11, 1979-80, pp. 59-64.

Protohistoric investigations in the Central Pennar Basin, Cuddapah District, Andhra Pradesh — **P.C. Venkata Subbaiah.** 18, 1987-88, pp. 79-84.

Puranic Lineages and Archaeological Cultures — **Romila Thapar.** 8, 1975-76, pp. 86-98.

Qutb Minar: Strengthening the Foundations— **R. Sengupta.** 10, 1978-79, pp. 70-75.

Rajghat Copper: A Metallurgical View — **H. C. Bhardwaj.** 2, 1968-69, pp. 30-34.

Rakta - Lokeśvara in Indian Buddhist Art — **Shashi Asthana.** 19, 1988-89, pp. 43-45.

Romano-Indian Rouletted Pottery in Indonesia —**J. Michael Walker and S. Santoso.** 9, 1977-79, pp. 104-108.

Ramayana: Some Problems Re-Examined — **K. D. Bajpai**. 10, 1978-79, pp. 76-78.

Rare Image of Avalokiteśvara from Eastern India — **Shashi Asthana.** 20, 1989-90, pp. 113-114.

Rare Object from Kosam — **Jayantika Kala.** 15, 1984-85, p. 120.

Readings in Indian Archaeology. 5, 1971-72, p. 104.

Recent Advances in Protohistoric Gujarat — **Suman Pandya.** 12, 1980-81, pp. 59-63.

Recent Advances in the Study of Indus Script — **Iravatham Mahadevan.** 9, 1977-78, pp. 34-42.

Recent Archaeological Activities in India — **D. Mitra.** 12, 1980-81, pp. 1-7.

Recent Archaeological Discoveries in North-Eastern India — **T.C. Sharma.** 7, 1974, pp. 17-19.

Recent Exploration in the Valley of Khari and Mansi Rivers, Rajasthan: with Special Reference to the Chalcolithic Sites — **B.R. Meena.** 16, 1985-86, pp. 17-23.

Regional Variations in the Indian Middle Stone Age Culture with Special Reference to Nalgonda in Andhra Pradesh — **S.N. Rao.** 2, 1968-69, pp. 13-15.

(The) Relationship between the Chalcolithic Culture of India and the Chust Culture of the Farghana Valley, USSR — **S.P. Gupta.** 1, 1967-68, pp. 47-53.

Report on the Chemical Analyses of the Glasses from Khairadih —**Ravindra N. Singh and A.A. Abdurajakov.** 21, 1990-91, pp. 92-96.

Reserved Slip Ware in the Harappan Context — **Dilip K. Chakrabarti.** 8, 1975-76, pp. 158-164.

Restoration of Angkor Vat (Cambodia): Indian Crusade — **B. Narasimhaiah.** 22, 1991-92, pp. 109-113.

Restrictions on Arresting Person: An Ancient Example — **R. Nagaswamy.** 17, 1986-87, pp. 31-32.

Rig-vedic Base of the Paśupati Seal of Mohenjo-daro — **S.P. Singh.** 19, 1988-89, pp. 19-26.

Rock-Engravings at Tabo, Distt., Lahul and Spiti, Himachal Pradesh — **A.K. Sinha.** 21, 1990-91, pp. 90-92.

Rock Pictures in Orissa — **Neumayer Erwin.** 22, 1991-92, pp. 13-24.

Role of Computer in Archaeology — **Aparna Sengupta**. 21, 1990-91, pp. 7-16.

Role of Temples in Medieval Orissa — **K.P. Padhy.** 21, 1990-91, pp. 85-86.

Role of the individual's perception and important explanatory models in Archaeology — **Vijneshu Mohan.** 21, 1990-91, pp. 51-56.

Role of Theory in the Study of Archaeology — **S.C. Malik.** 6, 1972-73, p. 1-11.

Rotary Quern Mining Industry at Kajachia, District, Panchmahals, Gujarat — **V.H. Sonawane.** 11, 1979-80, pp. 149-150.

Salvage Archaeology—Ahmadabad 1984 — **R.N. Mehta and Rasesh Jamindar.** 15, 1984-85, pp. 111 - 115.

Salvage of Archaeological Evidence from Bahadrabad — **Y.D. Sharma.** 5, 1971-72, pp. 39-42.

Sambara or Trailokyavijaya—Fresh identification — **J. Nath.** 17, 1986-87, pp. 57-58.

Sanghol Excavations 1987: Some New Evidence — **C. Margabandhu and G.S. Gaur.** 17, 1986-87, pp. 1-4.

Sankhu Buddha — **Balram Srivastava.** 1, 1967-68, pp. 85-86.

Saving a Great Asian Empire — **Asia Week Hong Kong.** 22, 1991-92, pp. 139-140.

Sculptural Art in Payar Temple — **Bansilal Malla.** 18, 1987-88, pp. 106-108.

Sealing from Sunet and Śaiva Vaishṇava Syncretism — **Kiran Kumar Thapliyal.** 3, 1969-70, pp. 74-76.

Session on NBP. — **D.P. Agrawal.** 5, 1971-74, pp. 34-35.

Session on NBP. — **M.N. Deshpande.** 5, 1971-72, p. 37.

Session on NBP. — **K.N. Dikshit.** 5, 1971-72, pp. 37-38.

Session on NBP. — **A. Ghosh.** 5, 1971-72, p. 38.

Session on NBP. — **R.C. Gaur.** 5, 1971-72, p. 34.

Session on NBP. — **N.C. Ghosh.** 5, 1971-72, p. 34.

Session on NBP. — **S.P. Gupta.** 5, 1971-72, pp. 35-36.

Session on NBP. — **M.C. Joshi.** 5, 1971-72, p. 36.

Session on NBP. — **Y.D. Sharma.** 5, 1971-72, p. 33.

Session on NBP. — **K.K. Sinha.** 5, 1971-72, p. 38.

Session on OCP. — **D.P. Agrawal.** 5, 1971-72, pp. 9-10.

Session on OCP. — **Ajay Mitra Shastri.** 5, 1971-72, pp. 21-24.

Session on OCP. — **N.R. Banerjee.** 5, 1971-72, p. 15.

Session on OCP.— **Suraj Bhan.** 5, 1971-72, pp. 16-21.

Session on OCP. (Inaugural Speech) — **M.N. Deshpande.** 5, 1971-72, pp. 5-7.

Session on OCP. — **M.N. Deshpande.** 5, 1971-72, pp. 26-27.

Session on OCP. — **K.N. Dikshit.** 5, 1971-72, pp. 8-9.

Session on OCP. — **A. Ghosh.** 5, 1971-72, pp. 27-28.

Session on OCP. — **R.C. Gaur.** 5, 1971-72, pp. 10-12.

Session on OCP. — **N.C. Ghosh.** 5, 1971-72, pp. 13-14.

Session on OCP. — **S.P. Gupta.** 5, 1971-72, pp. 7-8.

Session on OCP. — **M.C. Joshi.** 5, 1971-72, p. 13.

Session on OCP. — **Krishna Deva.** 5, 1971-72, pp. 15-16.

Session on OCP. — **R.S. Mittal.** 5, 1971-72, pp. 25-26.

Session on OCP. — **J.S. Nigam.** 5, 1971-72, p. 12.

Session on OCP. — **Shankar Nath.** 5, 1971-72, pp. 14-15.

Session on OCP. — **K.K. Sinha.** 5, 1971-72, pp. 24-25.

Session on OCP.— **L.M. Wahal.** 5, 1971-72, pp. 12-13.

Settlement Archaeology of Inamgaon— **M.K. Dhavalikar.** 8, 1975-76, pp. 44-54.

Settlement Archaeology of Kaothe: A Chalcolithic site in the Tapi Basin — **Vasant Shinde.** 22, 1991-92, pp. 47-52.

Ships and Shipping in Orissan Art — **J.K. Patnaik and B.K. Tripathy.** 23, 1992-93, pp. 61-63.

Siddhaikavira Image from Nalanda — **J. Nath.** 17, 1986-87, pp. 58-59.

Significance of Animal Fossils in the Prehistoric Studies of the Upper Mahanadi Valley, Central India — **R.P. Pandey.** 12, 1980-81, pp. 37-46.

Siswal: A pre-Harappan site in Drishadvati Valley — **Suraj Bhan.** 5, 1971-72, pp. 44-46.

Slip on Pottery: A Case Study — **D.K. Malik.** 11, 1979-80, pp. 164-165.

So-called Śyenachiti at Kausambi: A Fallen Brick Mass — **B.B. Lal.** 15, 1984-85, pp. 86-98.

Socio-economic Aspects of Megalithic Vidarbha — **Ravi Moorti.** 15, 1984-85, pp. 56-67.

Socio-Economic Note on Tribes and Peasants — **R.P. Sharma.** 6, 1972-73, pp. 60-63.

Sociological Framework for Archaeological Research — **Gopala Sarana.** 8, 1975-76, pp. 183-184.

Some Ancient sketches in Khajuraho Temples — **Deenabandhu Pandey.** 2, 1968-69, p. 59.

Some Aspects of Megalithic Culture of India — **H. Sarkar.** 11, 1979-80, pp. 49-55.

Some Aspects of the Archaeological Evidence Relating to the Indus Script — **B.B. Lal.** 7, 1974, pp. 20-24.

Some Aspects of the Chalcolithic Cultures of Central India — **M.K. Dhavalikar.** 4, 1970-71, pp. 24-30.

Some Fresh Evidence from Sanghol Excavations, 1986 — **C. Margabandhu and G.S. Gaur.** 16, 1985-86, pp. 73-78.

Some Indeterminate Terracotta objects-A study — **S. Jamal Hasan.** 10, 1978-79, pp. 104-105.

Some Literary References to Chinese Pottery in India — **K.K. Mohammed.** 11, 1979-80, pp. 78-80.

Some More Copper objects from Sheorajpur — **Suryakant Srivastava.** 19, 1988-89, pp. 70-71.

Some New Finds in Fatehpur District, Uttar Pradesh — **D.P. Sharma.** 11, 1979-80, pp. 65-67.

Some New Fossil discoveries from Western Maharashtra, India — **S.N. Rajaguru.** 2, 1968-69, pp. 16-20.

Some Rare Antiquities from Recent Excavation in Bihar — **B.P. Sinha.** 6, 1972-73, pp. 71-73.

Some Theoretical Aspects of Early Indian Urban Growth — **Dilip K. Chakrabarti.** 7. 1974, pp. 87-89.

Sringaverapura: A Key-site for the Protohistory and Early History of the Central Ganga Valley —**B.B. Lal and K.N. Dikshit.** 10, 1978-79, p. 1-7.

Status of Barley in Indian Archaeobotany with remarks on the Aryan Hypothesis — **Vishnu Mittre.** 3, 1969-70, pp. 1-2.

Stone Age Research in Kenojhar District, Orissa — **Pradeep Mohanty.** 17, 1986-87, pp. 54-55.

Stratigraphical Positon of the N.B.P. Ware in the Upper Ganga Basin and its Date — **M.D.N. Sahi.** 7, 1974, pp. 91-94.

Stratigraphy, Probable climatic phases and Dating of the Stone Age cultures of Upper Son Valley — **Nisar Ahmad.** 2, 1968-69, pp. 41-45.

Stuccos in Central Asia and India: A Reappraisal — **R. Sengupta.** 12, 1980-81, pp. 91-95.

Studies in Ancient Building Materials: A Note of Bhitari Plaster —**R.N. Singh and K.K. Jain.** 10, 1978-79, pp. 103-104.

Studies in Ancient Indian Technology: A Review — **H.C. Bhardwaj.** 13 & 14 1981-83, pp. 139-148.

Studies in the Archaeology and Palaeoanthropology of South Asia — **S.P. Gupta.** 12, 1980-81, pp. 169-172.

Study in the Stone age of Khajuraho in Central India — **Krishna Kumar.** 3, 1969-70, pp. 89-104.

Study of Place Names and Protohistoric Cultures in Andhra-Karnataka — **I.K. Sarma.** 11, 1979-80, pp. 56-58.

Study of the Iron Age in India — **Dilip K. Chakrabarti.** 13 & 14, 1981-83, pp. 81-85.

Stupas: A Rare Depiction in Rock Paintings of Gujarat, India — **V.H. Sonawane.** 23, 1992-93, pp. 66-69.

(A) Stylized Human-faced mask from a Megalithic Burial — **Nirmal Chandra Ghosh.** 6, 1972-73, pp. 74-75.

Subz-Burj: An Early Mughal Tomb — **M.C. Joshi.** 6, 1972-73, pp. 87-89.

Subsistence Pattern of an Early Farming Community of Western India — **M.K. Dhavalikar and Gregory L. Possehl.** 7, 1974, pp. 39-46.

Suggested Calssification of Northern Black Polished Ware — **T.N. Roy.** 10, 1978-79, pp. 106-109.

Sulabhdihi: A Neolithic Celt Manufacturing Centre in Orissa — **Pradip K. Behera.** 22, 1991-92, pp. 124-132.

Surkotada: A Chronological Assessment — **Jagat Pati Joshi.** 7, 1974, pp. 34-38.

Symbiosis and Traditional Behaviour in the Subsistence Economics of the Kunchapuri Yerukulas of South India: A Predictive Model — **M.L.K. Murty.** 10, 1978-79, pp. 50-61.

Taj Mahal – Some Issues of Conservation — **O.P. Agrawal.** 23, 1992-93, pp. 40-47.

Technical Examination of Some Medieval Glazed Wares from Fatehpur Sikri — **D.P. Agrawal, Kamal K. Jain and Tej Singh.** 17, 1986-87, pp. 50-53.

Techno-Typological Review of the Middle Palaeolithic Cultures of India —**Vidula Jayaswal.** 7, 1974, pp. 13-16.

(A) Technical Studies of Iron Implements from the Megalithic Site Tadakanhalli— **O.P. Agrawal, Harinarain and S.K. Bhatia.** 12, 1980-81, pp. 97-100.

Technology and Social Change in Early Indian History: A Note posing a Theorctical Question — **Niharranjan Ray.** 8, 1975-76, pp. 132-138.

(A) Terracotta Discs — **R.C. Gaur.** 10, 1978-79, pp. 100-101.

(A) Terracotta Medallion from Shahabad, District Hardoi, U.P.— **Jagdish Gupta.** 6, 1972-73, pp. 90-91.

Terracotta Medallion from Shahabad, District Hardoi, U.P. (Comments) — **M.C. Joshi.** 6, 1972-73, p. 91.

Thapli: A Painted Grey Ware site in Garhwal.— **K.P. Nautiyal and B.M. Khanduri** 10, 1978-79, pp. 94-95.

The Alleged Upper Palaeolithic Bone Mother Goddess from Belan — **S.P. Gupta.** 11, 1979-80, p. 116.

The Areca-nut object: is it a Bead? — **Peter Franics.** 10, 1978-79, pp. 95-99.

The Development of Eastern Bactria in Pre-Classical Times — **J. C. Gardin,** 10, 1978-79, pp. 8-13.

The Harappan Horse was buried under the dlunes of... — **A.K. Sharma.** 23, 1992-93, pp. 30-34.

Three Crystal Pendants of Identical Design — **P.K. Agrawala.**2, 1968-69, pp. 49-50.

Three Saucer-Type Coins from Varanasi — **Haldhar Pathak.** 16, 1985-86, pp. 89-90.

Timurid Mosque at Balkh in Afghanistan and Development of Mughal Domes in India— **R. Sengupta.** 9, 1977-78, pp. 57-63.

Trade Mechanisms in Indus-Mesopotamian Interrelations (Published in the Journal of the American Oriental Society, Vol. 92, No. 2, 1972) (Readings in Indian Archaeology — **Lamberg–Karlovsky, C.C.** 6, 1972-73, pp. 103-117.

Tribal deity of the Vishaṇins — **Deenabandhu Pandey.** 1, 1967-68, p. 99.

Two and half Million year old Human Skull found. (Press Cutting from the Motherland, Delhi, Nov. 1972) — **Richard Leakey.** 6, 1972-73, p. 113.

Two Early Stone Age Sites on River Son in District Bilaspur, M.P. — **Nisar Ahmad.** 1, 1967-68, pp. 87-89.

Two Earth-Works from Gujarat — **R.N. Mehta.** 3, 1969-70, pp. 54-57.

Two Relic-Caskets from Mathura — **P.K. Agrawala.** 3, 1969-70, pp. 49-52.

Two Urbanizations in India: A side Study in their Social Structure — **S.P. Gupta.** 7, 1974, pp. 53-60.

Typological Differences Between Indian and European Upper Palaeolithic Assemblages — **Tulika Banerjee.** 12, 1980-81, pp. 113-114.

Typological Variant within the Middle Paleolithic culture complex of India — **P. C. Pant and Vidula Jayasval:** 9, 1977-78, 78, pp. 15-33.

Typology in Prehistory — **P.C. Pant.** 1, 1967-68, pp. 61-67.

Unearthed Copper Antennae Sword of Tamil Nadu — **Devasahayam.** 12, 1980-81, p. 129.

Unique Art Relief frm Ajanta — **S.K. Mitra.** 22, 1991-92, pp. 133.

Unique Inscribed Metal sculpture of Padmapani from Western Himalayas — **A.K. singh, Ravindra N. Singh** and **Majula Chaturvedi.** 22, 1991-92, pp. 154-157.

Unique Pātravāhaka Yaksha Image from Achichchhatra — **Shashi Asthana.** 11, 1979-80, pp. 74-77.

Unique Terracota Figurine frm the Jorwe Levels of Daimabad — 5, **A. Sali.** 11, 1979-80, pp. 128-129.

University of Madras (Archaeology in Universities Series) T. V. Mahalingam. 2, 1968-69, pp. 61-62.

University of Saugar (Archaeology in Universities series) — **K.D. Bajpei.** 2.1968-69. pp. 63-64.

Upper Palaeolithic Culture in India — **Murty, M.L.K.** 10, 1978-79, pp. 50-61.Upper Palaeolithic Cultures of the Mid-son valley — **J.N. Pal.** 12, 1980-81, pp. 23-30.

Urban and Palace Water-works During the Mughal Period — **Khan, Mohd. Afral.** 19, 1988-89, pp. 46-49.

Urbanisation of Vaiśālī — **Sita Ram Roy.** 12, 1980-81, pp. 136-138.

Use of Arch in the Kushan Palace at Kausambi — **K.V. Soundara Rajan.** 11, 1979-80, pp. 96-102.

User of Caliche as a Chronological and Environmental Tool in the Study of Late Quaternary Formations in Gujarat and Rajasthan — **K.T.M. Hegde.** 8, 1975-76, pp. 37-43.

Use of Orthographic Projection in Archaeological Drawing — **S.S. Saar.** 12, 1980-81, pp. 159-161.

Use of the Terms 'Prehistory' and 'Protohistory' in Indian Archaeology — **K.K. Sinha.** 1, 1967-68, pp. 39-41.

Vaṅga and Vāhlika — **K.D. Bajpai.** 17, 1986-87, pp. 26-30.

Was Ayodhya a Mythical city? — **B.B. Lal.** 10, 1978-79, pp. 45-49.

When did Udayana rule? Ind the sixth century B.C. or the sixteenth century A.D.? An Assessment of the Dating of the Palace-Complex at Kausambi — **B. B. Lal.** 15, 1984-85, pp. 80-85.

World Archaeological Congress — **Jack Golson,** 21, 1990-91, pp. 99-101.

Writing Indian Art History. A search for valid approach — **S.P. Gupta.** 11, 1979-80, pp. 68-73.

OBITUARIES

Bajpai, K.D., 22, 1991-92, vii

Dales, George Franklin, 22, 1991-92, vii

Dasgupta, Paresh Chandra, Preliminary pages, 11, 1979-80.

Devahuti, 18, 1987-88, v

Ghosh, Amalananda, 10, 1978-79, ii

Krishnaswami, V.D., 4, 1970-71, i-iv

Sankalia, H.D., Preliminary pages, 19, 1988-89

Satya Prakash, Preliminary pages, 11, 1979-80

Seshadri, M. 6, 1972-73, Vii-viii

Sharma, G.R. 16, 1985-86, viii-ix

Singhal, D.P., 16, 1985-86, vii-viii

Sinha, K.K., 22, 1991-92, vii-viii

Varma, Kailash Chandra, 16, 1985-86, ix-x

From Gregory L. Possehl
The University of Pennsylvania Museum
University of Pennsylvania
33rd and Spruce Streets
Philadelphia, Pennsylvania
U.S.A. 19104-6324

November 18, 1994

Mr. T.D. Jogpal
Commissioner and Secretary
Department of Archaeology and Museums
State of Haryana
Chandigarh, INDIA

Thank you for your letter of 21-9-94 which arrived with eight charcoal samples from Kunal. I have had four of these samples processed at Beta Analytic, Inc. in Miami Florida. The samples that have been dated so far are:

Your S.R.	Date of Collection	Trench No.	Layer	Depth	BETA Number
2.	24.4.86	XA 3 I	12	243 cm	BETA-77728
3.	24.4.86	YA 2 II	10	300 cm	BETA-77727
4.	9.5.86	WC 2 II	3	75 cm	Too small for dating
5.	10.2.88	YC I IV	4	149 cm	BETA-77726

The dates we have been given for these samples are follows:

BETA No.	5568 Half life	5730 half life	Calibration by CALIB-3
BETA-77726	4040±70 bp	2210±75 bc	2837 (2568, 2519, 2504) 2466 cal. BC
BETA-77727	4250±130 bp	2430±135 bc	3016 (2884) 2621 cal. BC
BETA-77728	3990±70 bp	2160±75 bc	2577 (2473) 2409 cal. BC

Since these dates appear to be consistent and reasonable I am having the remaining four samples sent to Beta Analytic, Inc. assessment. They are smaller than the four samples submitted on the first round and it may be that they cannot be run."

INDIAN ARCHAEOLOGICAL SOCIETY

RECEIPTS AND PAYMENTS ACCOUNTS FOR THE YEAR ENDED 31-03-1994

Receipts		Payments	
By opening Balances:		To Honorarium	24575-00
		To Puratattva	44897-00
		To Conference Expenses	10475-00
Cash in hand	9573-86	To Furniture	952-00
Cash at Bank	155641-20	To Books	675-00
Fixed Deposit	1500000-00	To Typewriter	9200-00
By Grant Received from A.S.I.	24000-00	To Ground Rent paid to D.D.A.	23000-00
By Sale of Publication	10177-00	To Audit Fees	2250-00
By Life Membership Fees	3610-00	To Building Maintenance	265-00
By Membership Fees	610-00	To Printing & Stationery	6791-73
By Ord. Membership Fee	180-00	To Electricity & Water Charges	1234-00
By Bank Interest	256131-00	To Postage	2036-70
		To Conveyance	10145-04
		To Refreshment	522-30
		To Bank Charges	50-00
		To Misc. Expenses	1641-00
		To Cartage	408-00
		To Travelling Expenses	4617-00
		To Refund of Grant to National Museum	162500-00
		To Closing Balances	
		Cash in hand	148-09
		Cash at Bank	152930-20
		Fixed Deposits	1500000-00
	1959313-06		1959313-06

GENERAL SECRETARY

TREASURER

For Rajan Sharma & Co.,
Chartered Accountants.

Sd/-

(RAJAN KUMAR SHARMA)
Prop.

Place : New Delhi

Date : 1-11-1994

OFFICE BEARERS OF THE INDIAN ARCHAEOLOGICAL SOCIETY

Patrons :

Prof. B.B. Lal
F-7, Hauz Khas
New Delhi

Prof. B.P. Sinha
68, Pataliputra Colony
Patna

Chairman :

Dr S.P. Gupta
148, Vigyan Vihar
Delhi-110092.

Vice-Chairman :

Shri J.P. Joshi
Venus Co-operative Group Housing Society
Rohtak Road, Delhi

Prof. N.C. Ghosh
Viswa Bharati University
Shanti Niketan
West Bengal

General Secretary :

Shri K.N. Dikshit
B-322, Sarita Vihar,
New Delhi - 110044.

Hon. Treasurer :

Dr Shashi Asthana
Asstt. Director,
National Museum
New Delhi - 110011.

Secretary (Prehistory) :

Dr S.N. Rajaguru
Deccan College, Pune

Secretary (Protohistory) :

Dr Makkhan Lal
Aligarh Muslim University
Aligarh

Secretary (Historical Arch.) :

Prof. A. Sundara
Karnataka University
Dharwad

Secretary (Science) :

Prof. D.P. Agrawal
Physical Research Laboratory
Ahmedabad

Members of the Executive Committee :

Prof. P. Singh,
Banaras Hindu University,
Varanasi.

Dr V.D. Mishra,
Allahabad University,
Allahabad.

Dr V.H. Sonawane,
Baroda University,
Vadodara.

Dr R.C. Agrawal
Archaeological Survey of India,
Bhopal.

Prof. U.P. Arora
Rohalkhand University,
Bareilly.

Dr W.H. Siddiqui,
Raza Library,
Rampur.

Asstt. Secretary/Treasurer :

Shri Jitendra Nath
National Museum, New Delhi

Editor Monographs :

Shri K.S. Ramachandran
New Delhi

Headquarters:

INDIAN ARCHAEOLOGICAL SOCIETY
B-17, Institutional Area, Mehrauli, New Delhi – 110 016
Tel : S.P. Gupta/Shashi Asthana – 388067
K.N. Dikshit – 6828971